"We invite youth today to embark on their own unique gender journey. But imagine hiking into the wilderness without a map. Now, with the publication of *The Gender Quest Workbook*, Rylan Jay Testa, Deborah Coolhart, and Jayme Peta have provided just such a detailed topographical map for gender exploration. *The Gender Quest Workbook* is an invaluable resource for any youth wanting to explore their gender, and for the professionals and family members accompanying the youth on their venture. Just a generation ago, youth gender quests remained a topic of which we did not speak. *The Gender Quest Workbook* has broken that sound barrier by giving youth a place for their voice, inviting them to put words to their own journey as they engage in the exercises so brilliantly laid out by Testa, Coolhart, and Peta."

> —**Diane Ehrensaft, PhD**, director of mental health at the Child and Adolescent Gender Center, associate professor of pediatrics at the University of California, San Francisco, and author of *Gender Born, Gender Made* and *The Gender Creative Child*

"This workbook is an important resource for the transgender community. I wish I'd had something like it when I was coming out to myself."

> —**Greta Gustava Martela**, cofounder and executive director of Trans Lifeline, the first national crisis line for transgender people

"Informative, supportive, and fun. These playful and engaging exercises are powerful tools for self-discovery. I wish I'd had this guide as a teenager. Any young adult exploring gender will find freedom in these pages."

> —**Nick Krieger**, author of *Nina Here Nor There*

"The only book of its kind, *The Gender Quest Workbook* is an invaluable resource for transgender and gender-questioning youth, their families, the professionals in their lives, and anyone who is interested in 'undoing gender brainwashing.'"

—**Zander Keig, LCSW**, coeditor of *Letters for My Brothers* and *Manning Up*, and featured in the documentary *Zanderology*

"*The Gender Quest Workbook* is a wonderful new resource for exploring the evolving landscape of gender. Providing a road map for young people of any gender to examine their own experiences and understanding of this core aspect of self, this important tool also affirms the authenticity of individuals who find themselves in the less crowded terrain somewhere along the gender spectrum. Whether cisgender or gender expansive, more and more young people are personalizing their gender stories. *The Gender Quest Workbook* will play a critical role in shaping the narratives they create."

—**Joel Baum, MS**, senior director of professional development and family services at Gender Spectrum, and founding member and director of education and advocacy at the Child and Adolescent Gender Center at the University of California, San Francisco

"*The Gender Quest Workbook* is the perfect answer for anyone who is tired of textbooks and looking for a little fun! What better way to explore this topic than to get a chance to think about all the aspects of your gender in a step-by-step book."

—**Laura Erickson-Schroth, MD, MA**, psychiatrist and editor of *Trans Bodies, Trans Selves*

"*The Gender Quest Workbook* took me, a well-balanced adult transsexual, on a journey of gender discovery, showing me parts of myself I did not know existed. The overwhelming benefit of this kind of self-examination for our transgender youth is an utmost necessity for early identification. A positive future for our transgender children is greatly enhanced by teachers, clinicians, and parents utilizing this outstanding resource."

—**Rachael Rose Luckey**, filmmaker and transgender rights advocate

"*The Gender Quest Workbook* is an excellent resource for any young person who would like to explore gender. The authors really cover all the bases and bring to life the process by which a person can feel supported in bringing self-determination and creativity to expressing their gender. The language used is clear and user-friendly. I would absolutely recommend this to my clients. Testa, Coolhart, and Peta make excellent tour guides through this journey!"

—**Sand Chang, PhD**, clinical psychologist and gender specialist in the Kaiser Permanente Multi-Specialty Transitions Department, chair of the American Psychological Association (APA) Committee on Sexual Orientation and Gender Diversity (CSOGD), and coauthor of the APA *Guidelines for Psychological Practice with Transgender and Gender Nonconforming People*

the gender quest workbook

a guide for teens & young adults exploring gender identity

RYLAN JAY TESTA, PhD
DEBORAH COOLHART, PhD
JAYME PETA, MA

Instant Help Books
An Imprint of New Harbinger Publications, Inc.

Publisher's Note

This publication is designed to provide accurate and authoritative information in regard to the subject matter covered. It is sold with the understanding that the publisher is not engaged in rendering psychological, financial, legal, or other professional services. If expert assistance or counseling is needed, the services of a competent professional should be sought.

Distributed in Canada by Raincoast Books

Copyright © 2015 by Rylan Jay Testa, Deborah Coolhart, and Jayme Peta
Instant Help Books
New Harbinger Publications, Inc.
5674 Shattuck Avenue
Oakland, CA 94609
www.newharbinger.com

Cover design by Amy Shoup
Illustrations by Katja Tetzlaff and Julie Olsen
Cover photo by Ryan Donahoo @FreakMighty
Acquired by Tesilya Hanauer
Edited by Melanie Bell

Library of Congress Cataloging-in-Publication Data

Testa, Rylan Jay, author.
  The gender quest workbook : a guide for teens and young adults exploring gender identity / Rylan Jay Testa, PhD, Deborah Coolhart, PhD, Jayme Peta, MA, MS ; foreword by Ryan K. Sallans, M.A. ; afterword by Arlene Istar Lev, LCSW-R, CASAC.
      pages cm. -- (Instant help books)
  ISBN 978-1-62625-297-4 (pbk. : alk. paper) -- ISBN 978-1-62625-298-1 (pdf e-book) -- ISBN 978-1-62625-299-8 (epub) 1. Transgenderism--Juvenile literature. 2. Gender identity--Juvenile literature. 3. Sex differences (Psychology)--Juvenile literature. I. Coolhart, Deborah, author. II. Peta, Jayme, author. III. Title.
  HQ77.9.T47 2015
  306.76'8--dc23
                        2015032696

Printed in the United States of America

17   16   15

10   9   8   7   6   5   4   3   2   1   First Printing

This book is dedicated to all of those who embark on a Gender Quest. Your courage, creativity, and vision are changing how the world understands gender and creating pathways for transgender and gender expansive young people in the future.

contents

foreword

My first memory of gender, and what felt comfortable for me, took place when I was around three years old. It happened while I was standing outside, bare feet on the hot cement, next to a pool. I watched as my dad and brother were getting ready to jump into the clear blue water, shirtless. Their only clothing was small swimming trunks. As their bodies disappeared under the splashing water, I reached down and pulled off the top part of my two-piece bathing suit. I knew I should be wearing swim trunks; I knew I should be just like them. At that age, I didn't know how girls' and boys' bodies were different, but as my collection of Superman gear continued to grow, including action figures, cups, beach towels, kites, and coloring books, I began to realize I wasn't like the other boys. My body was a girl's body, and what people expected of me, because of this body, was different than what I wanted for myself.

When I was a teenager, I became really confused by all of the mixed messages I was getting both from the outside world and my internal self. Along with being confused by the fact that I didn't feel right in my gender, I was also extremely confused by whom I was attracted to. I dated and liked boys, but I also found that I had growing crushes on girls. I felt alone and scared, and I chose not to talk to anyone about my feelings. I kept everything bottled up inside, causing me to feel even more isolated from my family and friends.

I started to open up and take small steps in exploring my gender when I was in college. It began with writing a few sentences about my feelings of being a boy in my private journal, and then moved to me drawing pictures of myself as a boy in my sketchbook. When I was twenty-five years old, the word "transgender" became my reality after finding a book about transgender men in a bookstore. My quiet thoughts and private drawings shifted to me opening up to my therapist and friends, propelling my transition from female to male.

In looking back, I sometimes wonder what my life would have looked like if I had had the opportunity to think about gender when I was younger.

So here you are, holding a workbook that is going to allow you to do just that. Welcome to this journey; your very own Gender Quest. As you will find, there is so much to explore about what makes you…*you!* This includes what about your gender makes you the person that you are, and what outside your gender defines your personality, interests, and self.

This workbook is your private space to explore all of you, inside and out. You do not have to have all the answers going in, and you certainly do not need to have everything figured out when you are finished. This workbook can be revisited as many times as you need it. As a transgender man and professional speaker on gender, I have found that most people benefit from not trying to put themselves in one solidly-formed box. Even as adults, we continue to learn more about who we are relating to both our gender and our other identities.

Some parts of this workbook may be a little scary for you. Exploring who you are and finding that it is different from what your family, friends, or teachers think about who you are may make you feel confused or frightened. There are other emotions that may also come up, including anger, frustration, and sadness. I encourage you to sit with these feelings and try not to run away from them or let them defeat you. These feelings are normal and very important.

As you go through your Gender Quest, know that you are strong, you are not alone, and there are people around you that love you. If you are being bullied or if you are feeling alone, use this workbook to help you identify family, friends, teachers, or professionals that you can trust. Each step that you take in your life, the good, the average, and the bad, is worth it because each one teaches you a little more about what makes you unique—what makes you, *you.*

> —Ryan K. Sallans, M.A.
> Transgender Speaker, Educator, and Author
> Author, *Second Son: Transitioning Toward My Destiny, Love and Life*
> Omaha, NE

acknowledgments

All authors: We would like to thank the following organizations and people for their support and contributions: The Center for LGBTQ Evidence-Based Applied Research (CLEAR) at Palo Alto University; Gender Spectrum's Youth Council; Jennifer Orthwein, PhD, Esq.; Colton Keo-Meier, PhD; and Shane Hill, PhD.

Rylan Jay Testa, Ph.D.: I would personally like to thank Dr. Peter Goldblum for his irreplaceable mentorship and my incredible family and friends for their ongoing encouragement and support. Particular thanks goes to my two parents who exceed all reasonable expectations of what any parent hopes to be, providing genuine unconditional love and serving as inspiring role models.

Deb Coolhart, Ph.D., LMFT: I would like to acknowledge my kiddo, Jessy, and the supportive faculty and staff of Syracuse University's Marriage and Family Therapy program. I would also like to acknowledge all of the clients I have had the privilege to work with who expand, question, and transition gender; they continue to show me what courage looks like and challenge me to see the world in new and creative ways.

Jayme Peta, M.A., M.S.: I would like to thank Dr. Kimberly Balsam; my family, Nicolai, Denix, and Felix; and my parents. Your unwavering support, guidance, and encouragement mean everything to me.

introduction and outline

Congratulations! Because you had the interest and courage to open this book, you've gained immediate access to an exciting journey of self-discovery, called a Gender Quest!

"Um, what in the world is a Gender Quest?" you might ask.

Fair question! Let us tell you some more so you can decide if you would like to join us on this adventure.

First, what is the point of a Gender Quest?

We are taught many lessons from an early age about gender—what is masculine or feminine and how we should think, feel, and act accordingly. Yet, for many of us, what we are taught is not the whole story.

Many of us feel that our genders aren't fully explained by these lessons. For some of us, different questions may arise, like:

What gender am I?

What is gender, anyway?

What should I do if I feel my gender is different from what some other people think?

What do I do if my gender doesn't match my body?

The point of a Gender Quest is to help you answer these questions.

who is this book for?

This book is designed for teens and young adults who want to explore their gender or the concept of gender. This includes people who:

- have some questions about their gender identity

- want to explore different ways to express their gender

- feel pretty sure about their gender, but have questions about how to navigate their gender at home, school, work, or in relationships

- are considering making changes in their life to fit their gender better

- don't wish to make any changes at all but are courageously up for an exciting gender journey.

While it's not specifically designed for them, parts of this book might also be helpful for people who care about or are trying to better understand someone whose gender is different from how they usually think about gender.

who created this book?

This book is written by a group of people who have either gone through their own Gender Quests, or have helped others on their Gender Quests. We found these journeys to be fun, difficult, enlightening, and challenging. We wanted to see if we could pass on some of what we found helpful to other people bravely embarking on their own gender journeys.

what are the different parts of a gender quest?

Everyone has their own path to understanding their gender. You will likely find some of the chapters of this book super helpful and others, not as important for you.

For that reason, we'll go over the basics of the different chapters here, so you can decide which parts you want to dive into:

Chapter 1. Gender Identity

Explores definitions of gender and helps you better understand how your sense of gender developed.

Chapter 2. Gender Expression

Looks at the wide diversity of genders worldwide and helps you think about the different ways you may choose to express your gender.

Chapter 3. Family

Explores how to navigate your gender in your family.

Chapter 4. School and Work

Discusses how to advocate for yourself, find support, and tackle some common gender-related challenges at school and work.

Chapter 5. Friends and Other Peers

Explores how you might communicate with friends, classmates, and coworkers about gender.

Chapter 6. Dating and Sex

Talks about sexual and romantic identities, dating, and sex.

Chapter 7. Balancing Multiple Identities

Explores how our multiple identities (ethnic, socioeconomic, religious, and so on) combine to form who we are as unique and whole people.

Chapter 8. Dealing with the Hard Stuff

Describes how to deal with any stressful challenges that come up on your Gender Quest.

There is just so much cool stuff you can do on a Gender Quest, we couldn't fit it all in the book. So you can also go to this website (http://www.newharbinger.com/32974) to get a super useful list of resources, as well as a guide for clinicians and other support people working with you.

Resources

Our list of resources offers further ways to connect with information, people, and support that may be helpful to you. Specific suggestions are provided related to online support, medical or social transition, health, people of color, therapists, crisis, fiction and nonfiction books, conferences, family members and allies, schools, religion and spirituality, and policy and legal issues.

Supplemental Guide for Clinicians

This workbook is also designed to be used as a clinical resource for therapists and counselors working with individuals facing questions, conflict, or challenges related to gender identity or expression. Clinicians considering using this workbook or parts of it with any client will benefit from accessing this supplemental guide online.

Finally, we want you to know that you don't have to go on a Gender Quest alone. Sometimes, adventures are even more fun with company. If you have a friend or anyone else you trust to go through this book with you, great. If you have a therapist or counselor or can find one who you trust to go along with you, wonderful. Otherwise, don't fret, we'll be by your side throughout your journey!

chapter 1

gender identity

What is gender, anyway?

To give a very complicated question a simple answer, gender is both (1) how you express masculinity, femininity, or for most people, some mix of the two and (2) how your identity, or sense of self, relates to masculinity and femininity. Gender can be expressed in how you style your hair, what clothes you wear, how your voice sounds, or even through what hobbies you choose. In our view, there are about as many different gender identities as there are people. The options are infinite. It seems that even the people who appear most comfortable in their gender still have their own nuanced feeling for what it means to be them. And figuring that out, well, that's a Gender Quest.

Gender is a confusing topic for most of us. Here are just a few of the questions the authors have answered over the years:

How is gender different from sex?

Has gender always been around? Will it always be around?

If I move to Jupiter, will gender exist there?

Do all animals have genders?

How many genders are there?

Can a person's gender change over time?

Does your gender come from how you're raised? Or is it from your genes or brain?

In the space that follows, write some questions you have about gender. Don't be shy; this is a space to say whatever comes to mind.

_____

_____

_____

_____

_____

_____

Answers to any of these questions aren't simple. Gender is actually a pretty complicated and interesting thing. Let's take a look...

the difference between gender and sex

In mainstream American culture, "gender" is often equated with "sex." Even when people do know these two words mean different things, they may be confused about how.

sex

The word "sex" is tricky itself, because it is used to describe two very different things. Sex can be used to talk about:

1. physical intimacy between people ("what happens between the sheets")

or to refer to

2. whether someone is "male," "female," or "intersex" ("what's between the legs").

It is this second definition, relating to the words "male," "female," and "intersex," that people often think of as being the same as "gender." But guess what? It's not! Sex and gender are different things!

more about sex

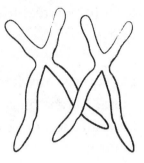

Many people think that all mammals, including humans, naturally come in one of two varieties—males or females. They also think it is simple to tell who goes in which category. Many kids are taught that the difference between males and females is whether or not the person has a penis or a vagina. When people get older and take some biology classes, they may think that the difference is in sex chromosomes (part of your genes). We are taught that males have the genes XY, whereas females have the genes XX. Notice that in both cases, whether we are talking about genitals or chromosomes, there are only two options—male or female.

Few people are told the truth about sex—that nature doesn't fall neatly into these categories. In fact, many healthy babies are born with genitals that are not clearly "male" or "female" (intersex babies). Some people are born with genes different from XY or XX (like XXY, for example). There are also people whose genes and genitals don't "match" as expected (like people with XY genes who have a vagina). Finally, even people who are not intersex often have some characteristics that we would consider unusual for their sex. When people grow up, their bodies produce hormones, and they develop "secondary sex characteristics" like facial and body hair, deepening voice, breasts, wider hips, or more muscle mass. We usually think about things like facial hair as being a "male-only thing" and things like breasts as being a "female-only thing." But actually, many people with penises develop some breast tissue, and many people with vaginas develop some facial hair. All perfectly natural. Just not widely talked about.

Try It Out!: sex characteristics—test your sex vision

Find a time and place in your day when you can do some people watching. You can observe people walking by on the street, shopping, or playing outside. They shouldn't be people on television shows or movies, since these people are often selected and made up to look a certain way. Give yourself time to observe at least fifteen real-life females and fifteen real-life males and answer the following questions:

Do you see any females who have some biological traits we usually categorize as male? Maybe bigger muscles on their arms, a deeper voice, thinner hips, some hairs on their face, or other examples? Write what you find:

_____

_____

_____

_____

What about the males? Do they have any traits we usually categorize as female? Maybe some of them are shorter than most males? Do you notice any who don't have much hair on their bodies or face, who have a higher voice, wider hips, some breast tissue, or other examples?

_____

_____

_____

_____

Did you notice yourself judging any of these people's traits as good, bad, pretty, handsome, or ugly? Most of us have been taught that having masculine traits is good if you are a man, but bad if you are a woman, and similarly, that having feminine traits is good if you are a woman and bad if you are a man. In fact, after learning this lesson, some people go to great lengths, spending time and money to remove hair, add hair, remove breasts, get bigger breasts, gain muscle, lose weight, and so on, all to look more like what they are taught they are supposed to look like based on their sex.

Do you know anyone who does these things? Or have you tried any of these things? Write any examples here:

_____

_____

_____

_____

_____

So to sum it up, sex has to do with *biology*. From what you wrote down above, you can probably see that sex doesn't fall into two neat categories. Instead, sex is the biology of how male, female, both, neither, or in-between someone is.

gender

Gender is a very different thing from sex. Gender isn't "what's between your legs," it's "what's between your ears." In other words, gender is how you think and feel about yourself, and how you behave or express yourself in the world. You cannot tell a person's gender from their biology. Instead of talking about whether someone is "male" or "female," we most often use the words "man/boy" or "woman/girl" when referring to someone's gender. Many people think if someone has a penis that means they must be a man or boy. This is not true. When a person is born with a penis the doctors may shout, "It's a boy!" but what they actually mean is that this person's sex is male.

9

How do you know if you are a boy, a girl, or another gender?

And how do you know what gender someone else is if you can't see it?

Well, here's a puzzle for you to solve:

If a girl went to a magician who mistakenly had her vagina turn into a penis, would she suddenly become a boy?

No! She would still know she was a girl. Just a girl with a penis.

Another puzzle:

If a boy lost a really big bet and had to dress and act "like a girl" for the rest of his life, would he become a girl?

No! He would still be a boy. Just a boy in a dress who was acting "like a girl."

As mentioned above, gender has to do with both how you think and feel about yourself (called your "gender identity") and how you behave or express yourself in the world (called "gender expression").

gender identity

Because people have all sorts of thoughts and feelings about their genders, people have all sorts of gender identities. For example, a person may identify as a man, woman, transgender man, transgender woman, genderqueer, bigender, Two-Spirit, or something very unique and creative, like a "gender Prius," "gender Oreo," or "gender swirl."

Here are how some of the more common gender identities are usually defined:

Agender: Someone who identifies as having no gender.

Androgynous: A person who has both masculine and feminine traits. This may also be used to refer to a person whose gender is hard to determine visually.

Bigender: Some people use this word to describe themselves as switching gender in different contexts. One example is someone who is very masculine at their welding class, but loves to dress in heels and a skirt to go out to a club.

Cisgender: This refers to someone whose gender identity and expression is a good match for their natal sex. They appear to fit cultural expectations of what a "man" or "woman" should look and act like. Some also say "gender normative."

Cross-Dresser: This refers to someone who, in specific situations, wears clothes, makeup, hairstyle, and so on that are usually reserved for another gender. While this identity is sometimes put under the "transgender" umbrella, often cross-dressers do not identify as transgender. Some people cross-dress as part of performance ("drag queens" and "drag kings"). The word "transvestite," often used to describe a person who cross-dresses, is considered offensive.

Female to Male / FTM / F2M / Trans Man: This is a person who was assigned the sex "female" at birth and has transitioned socially, physically, or both to live as a man. Some refer to themselves as "trans men," as it can sound a little less "clinical."

Gender Diverse / Gender Expansive: Those who don't conform to the expectations that society has for their gender. Many prefer this over "gender variant," which implies that those who don't identify with society's expectations are "abnormal."

Gender Fluid: Some people identify as gender fluid to describe a sense that they are comfortable with a shifting and changing notion of their own gender. They do not feel that their gender identity is "fixed."

Gender Nonconforming: This describes a person whose gender doesn't conform to societal expectations based on their natal sex. Similar to "gender diverse" or "gender expansive."

Genderqueer: Those who identify as genderqueer feel that their primary sense of felt gender is neither "male" nor "female" but somewhere in between.

Male to Female / MTF / M2F / Trans Woman: This is a person who was assigned the sex "male" at birth and has transitioned socially, physically, or both to live as a woman. Some refer to themselves as "trans women," as it can sound a little less "clinical."

Natal Sex / Natal Gender: The sex or gender that was assigned to you at your birth. Some say "birth sex" or "birth gender." This is preferable to "biological" sex because for many transgender people, quite a bit about their "biology" has changed over time through use of hormones, surgeries, and other aspects of transition. We also don't say "genetic sex" because very few of us have had our genetics tested to confirm our assumptions that we don't have a genetic variation.

Pangender: Those who identify as pangender embrace all genders in their identity. They reject the notion that there are only two genders.

Transfeminine: Those who were assigned male at birth, but now identify as transgender and more strongly with the "feminine" end of the gender spectrum.

Transgender: This is a term that can apply to all people for whom their current gender identity is different from what would be expected from them by society. This can include those who have chosen to physically or socially transition and those who have not. Remember, even though the term "transgender" is often used alongside the terms "lesbian," "gay," and "bisexual" (as in LGBT), transgender is a gender identity, not a sexual orientation!

Transmasculine: Those who were assigned female at birth, but now identify as transgender and more strongly with the "masculine" end of the gender spectrum.

Two-Spirit: This is an identity that is specific to those in indigenous North American cultures. Indigenous Americans belong to a diverse number of cultures, each of which has a different understanding of gender. However, this is a general term used by some Native Americans to describe those who have gendered appearances or identities other than "male" or "female."

gender expression

Gender expression also can't be divided into two simple categories. Gender expression is how we present ourselves in the world, including how we carry ourselves, dress, and talk. In mainstream American culture, we tend to recognize certain behaviors and traits, such as wrestling and assertiveness, as "masculine," and other behaviors and traits, such as wearing makeup and being caring, as "feminine." Of course, people of all gender identities have behaviors and traits that are considered masculine and considered feminine. Thank goodness, since ideally all people could be both assertive and caring! But when we sum together a person's behaviors, we may think they end up high or low on either scale.

Try It Out!: gender expression

Choose two family members and two friends. Where do you think each falls on the following scales of gender expression—femininity and masculinity? Notice people can be high on both or low on both scales at the same time.

Family Member 1: _____

Femininity:

None   A Whole Ton

Masculinity:

None   A Whole Ton

Family Member 2: _____

Femininity:

●——●
None   A Whole Ton

Masculinity:

●——●
None   A Whole Ton

Friend 1: _____

Femininity:

●——●
None   A Whole Ton

Masculinity:

●——●
None   A Whole Ton

Friend 2: _____

Femininity:

●——●
None   A Whole Ton

Masculinity:

●——●
None   A Whole Ton

undoing gender brainwashing

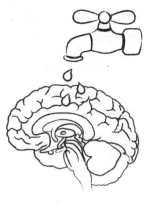

Like we've been saying, we are all taught certain lessons about gender, like how many genders there are and what someone of a particular gender should look like or act like. When everyone is taught these same lessons, it can seem like they're facts. But as we look at the realities of people's appearances and their experiences, we begin to realize that our beliefs about gender are not based on fact. We realize... Hey! We've been gender brainwashed!

The bad news is, being gender brainwashed can really put a stop to a Gender Quest. If we keep relying on our old knowledge that tells us that there are two sexes, and that all females should be pretty, polite girls and all males should be strong, domineering boys—well, there's really not much to explore. If we are to have any hope of truly understanding gender, we have to find a way to undo our gender brainwashing.

The good news is we found a way to undo the gender brainwashing. First we have to explore the lessons we've been taught. Then we have to examine what different stories are out there about gender. This will let us begin to form our own, more informed beliefs. You can get started with the activities that follow.

Try It Out!: gender ideas

Let's start by examining your gender beliefs. When you rated your family members and friends in the last activity, how did you know what to classify as masculine and feminine? Have you learned ideas about gender from the people and images around you? Write down some ideas you have been taught about what is masculine and feminine below:

_____

_____

_____

_____

What have all of these lessons taught you about what is masculine? Draw a picture of what comes to mind below:

What have all of these lessons taught you about what is feminine? Draw a picture of what comes to mind below:

As we mentioned earlier, not only does mainstream American culture teach us certain lessons about what is masculine or feminine; it also teaches us that it is "good" when females are women and feminine, and when males are men and masculine. This idea that people fall into two boxes is an overly simple understanding. Picture males, men, and masculinity all squished to one side of the spectrum with a box drawn around them, and females, women, and femininity all squished to the other side, in their own box.

We get so used to these boxes of male/men/masculine and female/women/feminine that it is often shocking to realize they don't really exist! But in fact, there are many examples of entirely different understandings of gender.

For example, many Native American tribes recognize three or more genders. And the modern term "Two-Spirit" is used by many Native American people who do not identify as men or women. Two-Spirited individuals traditionally held roles of distinction within their tribes and were often shamans. There are numerous other examples across the globe, including the Katoey or "ladyboys" of Thailand, the Salzikrum of the Middle East, the Hijra caste of India, the Fa'afafine of Samoa, the Travestis of South America, the Burrnesha of Albania, and the Muxhe of Southern Mexico. Breaking the gender binary has occurred all over the world throughout history!

Try It Out!: gender across history and time

We barely scratched the surface with our examples above. It's your turn to explore this topic on your own. An easy way to begin is simply to search the Internet. Try searching some of the peoples we mentioned above, or search under topics like "third gender," "transgender people in Thailand," or "transgender people in history." Look up different countries, historical times, and eras. American history also has its own rich history of transgender individuals. If you are not much into Internet research, and even if you are, we encourage you to check out this book too: *Transgender Warriors: Making History from Joan of Arc to Dennis Rodman* by Leslie Feinberg. Individuals who defy the gender binary are woven throughout history. You simply have to look to find them!

Did you research the presence of a third/fourth/fifth gender within different cultures? What did you find?

_____

_____

_____

Have you found any individuals who have defied the gender binary? What was it like to discover the story of these individuals?

_____

_____

_____

Try It Out!: gender interview

While mainstream American culture continues to hold the two gender boxes, gender roles have changed immensely over the past fifty years.

Find a woman you know who is over fifty and grew up in a culture similar to yours. Ask her: "What has changed for women over your lifetime?" Take some notes below. If she isn't sure what you mean, ask her whether it is acceptable for women now to do different things, wear different things, work different jobs, or have a different role in a family than when she was born.

_____

_____

_____

_____

Ask the same questions of a man you know who is over fifty and grew up in a culture similar to yours, and write your notes here:

_____

_____

_____

_____

You may see in your notes that cultural expectations for gender expression do change in a culture over time. Recently, people have become more visible who not only break societal rules about gender, but who also make society question its boxes. The visibility of gender diversity in mainstream American culture continues to shift our understanding of gender. Let's hear from some people who are on the forefront of this knowledge:

Prior to the birth of my two kids I was a pediatric nurse. Now I am a stay-at-home dad and I have never been happier. People often make comments about the supposed role reversal in our home but for the most part they are easily ignored. I have always been most comfortable in the "caregiver" role while my wife greatly enjoys her career as a corporate attorney. We are happy in our roles and that is what is important to us.

I love both my feminine and masculine sides. I am just as comfortable in a dress as I am on the football field.

Dressing in drag is my escape. I am a handsome gay man by day and a beautiful drag queen by night. I am comfortable as a man and in no way want to be a woman, but I love being a drag queen.

When I was a little "girl," my parents said I refused to play with dolls and just hated pink. I would only wear boy clothes. So, it wasn't a surprise to them when I announced I was a boy at seven, and later, at eighteen, started to physically transition to be a man.

My sister tells me that I loved hanging out with her friends when I was a really young boy, and that I didn't get into "boy stuff" in middle school. When I was in college, I realized I was much happier as a woman. Now, I'm pretty feminine but love that I can change the oil on my car.

So how does your brain feel? Are you still stuck in your gender brainwashing, or is it beginning to come undone? If you find that your ideas about gender are getting more complicated or confusing, or are starting to be more clear, or are changing in any way at all, then congratulations! You are starting to break free of gender brainwashing!

exploring your gender identity

Now that we know a bit about what gender is, let's take a look at our own gender identities.

Remember, gender identity is what is on the inside, "between your ears," and separate from gender expression (things on the outside that others can see).

How do I know what gender I am?

Because gender identity is on the inside, that means you are the only one who can determine what your gender identity is. For some that feels good to hear, because no one else can control their identity. However, if you are feeling a bit confused about your gender, it can also be a little scary to hear you are the only one who can figure it out. The good news is, you don't have to figure it out alone. That's why we're here!

Is there a test I can take?

Nope. Some people wish there were a test. They may think it would be easier to get others to accept them, or even to figure things out themselves, if there were. But no worries! We have designed some activities below to help you find out more about your gender identity.

Try It Out!: my gender

To explore your inner thoughts and feelings about gender, get in a safe, quiet space so you can answer the following questions as honestly as possible.

What are some of your earliest memories related to gender? (For example: *I remember my dad saying, "Are you sure you don't want a blue balloon? Blue is for boys."* Or, *I remember wanting to be in Boy Scouts like my brother, but my parents said I couldn't because I was a girl.*)

_____

_____

_____

_____

_____

Were you ever told you looked or acted like a boy? Like a girl? How did you feel when this happened?

_____

_____

_____

_____

_____

How would it or does it feel when people see you as a boy or man?

(A note for this question and the next two: Sometimes when you imagine these scenarios, the first thing you feel is fear. Fear can overshadow other emotions. So if you feel fear, write that down, but then put down what other emotions you would feel after that. It may help to think of this happening in a special situation where there would be no possible danger or rejection.)

_____

_____

_____

_____

_____

How would it or does it feel when people see you as a girl or woman?

_____

_____

_____

_____

How would it or does it feel when people see you as a gender other than girl/woman or boy/man (for example, as androgynous or Two-Spirit)?

_____

_____

_____

_____

_____

Who are your gender role models? In other words, if you could be like anyone in terms of gender, who would you be like?

_____

_____

_____

_____

_____

Fold a piece of paper in half, like a book. Draw on the cover of this book how you think other people see your gender. Now open the book. Draw how you see your gender, or how you would like the world to see your gender. If they are different, draw both on different sides of the inside of your book. How do you feel when you look at each version of yourself?

_____

_____

_____

_____

_____

Read the following examples. Underline parts of people's experiences that feel "right on" to you. Cross out parts that feel different from your experience. Some parts won't have an underline or a cross; they will just be neutral or unsure, and that is fine.

My whole life I felt like something just wasn't right. Sometimes I would look in the mirror and feel like I was looking at someone else. Like it wasn't me. The person I saw in the mirror and the person I felt I was were not the same.

I love to be surprising: I make sure that people know that even though they see me as a girl, I love sports. Or, if they think I'm a "tomboy," that I also have a huge number of dresses.

As a child it never really crossed my mind that I was transgender. I seemed to like all the same things that the other boys liked. I liked sports and I liked girls. It was not until high school that I started to think that my experience was different. It is hard to describe how I felt or why I felt that way but I just did not feel like a guy. When I say that I am a woman it feels right. I feel like I have always been a woman and not much has really changed. I still like sports and I still like girls.

I've spent a lot of time trying to prove to people that I'm not gay. As hard as I try, though, people always seem to notice that I'm more feminine than other guys. My parents criticize me a lot for this.

I love being a girl and I always have!

I always hated dresses. I hated dolls. I hated Barbies. I preferred playing with all my brother's toys and never touched my own. As a kid my mom would always say I was a tomboy and tell my dad that I would outgrow it. I never did. There never came a time when I wanted to wear a dress or paint my nails. I never really cared or thought about whether I was a girl or a boy until I was around twelve years old. My body started to change and I did not like it. It felt wrong, like something was happening that I could not control. Something I did not want.

I never really felt like a boy, but I never really felt like a girl either. I just wish I could move somewhere that gender doesn't exist and be me—not a boy or a girl.

Kids at school always make fun of me for acting "like a girl." The truth is, I do kind of feel more like a girl than a boy. But it's hard to say that.

I'm a total boy and that's just me. But I also really like that I was raised a girl when I was younger. I think it made me better able to understand different perspectives.

Now combine all the parts of the above experiences that felt "right on" to you and write them below:

_____

_____

_____

_____

_____

_____

Does this represent your experience? What is missing?

_____

_____

_____

summary

In this chapter we covered a ton of information. While it may seem a bit overwhelming now, remember you can come back and review it at any time. In fact, we encourage you to revisit this chapter later in your quest and see if you still feel the same. For now, let's take a few minutes and reflect on your journey so far.

What did you learn from this chapter or what stuck out the most?

_____

_____

_____

Did you discover anything about yourself? What?

_____

_____

_____

How do you feel about your discovery? Are you surprised? Confused? Relieved?

_____

_____

_____

What questions do you still have?

_____

_____

_____

chapter 2

gender expression

(additional contributing author: Jennifer Hastings, MD)

Congratulations on getting this far! You now know a lot more than most people about gender!

So far, your Gender Quest has been a journey into what you feel like on the inside. But that of course leads to the next question: *What does that mean about how I look on the outside?*

As we said in chapter 1, *gender expression* is how people present their gender to the world. Since all sorts of things are seen as related to gender, gender expression can include how you walk, dress, talk, gesture, wear your hair—the list is endless.

This chapter will guide you in exploring the many ways gender can be expressed, how others express gender, and how you would like to express your gender. We'll ask you to do some observations and experiments. As always, you should not do anything you feel is too unsafe or uncomfortable for you. At the same time, know that while thinking about and trying on gender expressions can be a little uncomfortable for anyone, that doesn't mean it won't be fun or exciting too!

my past gender adventures

When we are young, before we are taught that certain ways of dressing, talking, walking, and acting are okay and others are not, we often feel more free to experiment with different ways to look. Maybe you played dress up, put on costumes for Halloween, used markers to make "nail polish," put a bandanna over your face to be a cowboy, used towels to make pretend hair, or wore your dad's shirts and ties to pretend to go to work. One of the authors' dads would put shaving cream on his kids to make it look like the white beard of an old man! Maybe you did a bunch of these things on the same day. All of this is part of the normal exploration of self-expression that all kids go through.

Try It Out!: my past gender adventures

When you were younger, what ways did you experiment with your self-expression? List at least three times you remember experimenting with gender and what you did. Then list how you felt, and if others saw you, what that was like.

Age _____

What you did _____

How you felt _____

_____

_____

Age _____

What you did _____

How you felt _____

_____

_____

Age _____

What you did _____

How you felt _____

_____

_____

Age _____

What you did _____

How you felt _____

_____

_____

What did you think about yourself as a result of these instances?

_____

_____

_____

_____

 ## observing gender

Now that you're older, there may be more things you consider when expressing your gender. For example, you might wonder: *What would my friends think if I did that? What would my parents say if I did that? What about other people? Is that safe for me to do? Is that even possible for me to do?*

All this wondering can get very stressful! And some people may even want to abandon their Gender Quest!

But we know that if you have gotten this far, you have what it takes for a Gender Quest. And we are here to help you figure out what will be both safe and satisfying for you.

So get ready—time for your next journey!

Just like you did when you were younger, experimenting with your appearance can help you get a sense of how you are most comfortable with your gender expression. Some people might assume we're just talking about clothes or makeup but there are actually a whole lot of ways you can play around with self-expression—especially when it comes to gender!

Try It Out!: searching for gender

Where is gender? Well, once you start looking, it turns out it's just about everywhere! Let's see what you can find.

In chapter 1, we did some people watching to observe biological characteristics, like body shape or hairiness. This time we are going to do another half hour of people-watching to observe behaviors related to gender, such as clothes people wear, how they style their hair, whether they wear makeup or nail polish, and their body language. You can go watching anywhere you can see a lot of people—at a coffee shop, on the street, at school, or in a mall. (Just remember to blink occasionally—we don't want your eyes drying out or anything!) You can go several places if you think you might look suspicious staying in one spot. Afterwards, answer the following questions:

What are the different things you see that go into people's gender expression?

_____

_____

_____

_____

Focus for a little while on the people you saw as "girls" or "women." Did all of them express gender in the same way? Write down some ways these people showed feminine, masculine, and neutral gender expressions:

Feminine:

_____

_____

Masculine:

_____

_____

Neutral:

_____

_____

Now let's focus on the "boys" or "men." Did all of them express gender in the same way? Write down some ways these people showed feminine, masculine, and neutral gender expressions:

Feminine:

_____

_____

Masculine:

_____

_____

Neutral:

_____

_____

Now that your eyes made it through the half hour, think back over your observations. What ways of expressing gender did you find yourself admiring? Remember, no judgment here in this book, so write as honestly as possible.

_____

_____

_____

Now let's put our heads together. Here are some forms of self-expression and style we've seen on people of different genders. Did we miss any? If so, fill them in below:

- Hair: Long, short, spiky, colored, curly, straight, braided, pulled back

- Clothes: Funky, conservative, floral prints, ties

- Shoes: Boots, heels, flip-flops, oxfords, tennis sneakers, flats

- Jewelry: Earrings, cuff links, piercings, necklaces, watches

- Fingernails and toenails: Polished, plain, long, short

- Scent: Fruity, musky, floral

- Makeup: Subtle, dramatic, none

- Glasses: None, thick-rimmed, sunglasses, sparkly

- Body language: Swaggering, delicate, confident, flirty

- _____

- _____

- _____

Many people are surprised to find the huge variety in gender expression that's just a part of everyday life. You may have discovered guys wearing floral prints or necklaces. Or you might have seen that you don't need to be a "guy" to have short hair or a masculine walk. Your gender expression is just that: yours.

expressing yourself beyond gender

So we know we keep saying gender is everywhere, but that doesn't mean it is everything! When you observed people, I bet you noticed that people's presentations can fall along a few different spectrums. Look at the different spectrums below.

Casual	————————————————	Fancy
Funky	————————————————	Conservative
Fashionable	————————————————	Traditional
Gender-neutral	————————————————	Feminine
Gender-neutral	————————————————	Masculine

For example, on a Monday morning one transgender girl dresses for school in jeans and a cute sparkly T-shirt, leaves her hair long and down, wears no makeup, no jewelry, and has fun sneakers with big colorful laces. She is quiet and soft-spoken in class. She is very athletic and plays on the soccer team. So, on this Monday morning at school we might see her self-expression like this:

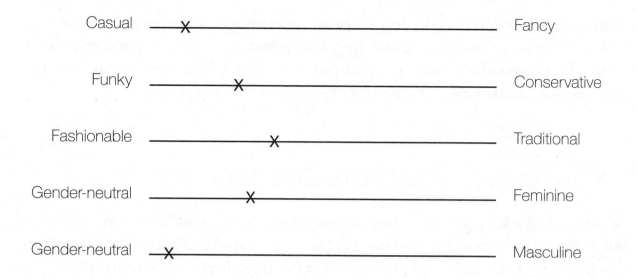

Now this is just how we might see her on one Monday morning. If she changes clothes for soccer practice, or changes how loud and assertive she is when she is home with her family, we might put the Xs in different places then. *Remember that just because her gender expression changes, this doesn't mean her gender identity changes. Dressing and talking differently can only change how you appear, not who you are!*

Try It Out!: What I Show the World

How do you think you present yourself on a typical day at school or work?

Casual _____ Fancy

Funky _____ Conservative

Fashionable _____ Traditional

Gender-neutral _____ Feminine

Gender-neutral _____ Masculine

At a party?

Casual _____ Fancy

Funky _____ Conservative

Fashionable _____ Traditional

Gender-neutral _____ Feminine

Gender-neutral _____ Masculine

On a weekend when you are hanging around at home?

Casual _____ Fancy

Funky _____ Conservative

Fashionable _____ Traditional

Gender-neutral _____ Feminine

Gender-neutral _____ Masculine

Now let's think about a dream scenario. Imagine if in all of the places below, no matter how you dressed or acted, everyone would be totally accepting. If this were true, how would you like to dress and present yourself?

School:

_____

_____

_____

The grocery store:

_____

_____

_____

Dinner with someone you're interested in:

_____

_____

_____

Out with friends on Saturday afternoon:

_____

_____

_____

A fancy event like prom or a wedding:

_____

_____

_____

The gym:

_____

_____

_____

A hike or bike ride:

_____

_____

_____

How did you feel imagining these situations? It is natural that some thoughts came up like *I'd love to but my friends would…* or *My mother would never let me…* It is also natural to feel a whole assortment of feelings, from scared and nervous to surprised and excited.

Pick the three places above where you spend the most time, and fill them in the blanks below. Then tell us how you thought and felt about each.

When I thought about how I might dress for _____ I thought to myself:

_____

_____

_____

I felt:

Excited	Happy	Glad
Curious	Surprised	Worried
Nervous	Angry	Eager
Sad	Frustrated	Unhappy
Relieved	Joyful	Embarrassed

When I thought about how I might dress for _____ I thought to myself:

_____

_____

_____

I felt:

Excited	Happy	Glad
Curious	Surprised	Worried
Nervous	Angry	Eager
Sad	Frustrated	Unhappy
Relieved	Joyful	Embarrassed

When I thought about how I might dress for _____ I thought to myself:

_____

_____

_____

I felt:

Excited	Happy	Glad
Curious	Surprised	Worried
Nervous	Angry	Eager
Sad	Frustrated	Unhappy
Relieved	Joyful	Embarrassed

getting ready to experiment with gender

There are a lot of ways to begin to experiment with gender. First, you may wish to do some planning about when, where, and how you'd like to experiment. For example, you might like to think about trying on some makeup. When would it make sense to try this out? With whom? In what type of place?

In many places in the United States, if you are mostly seen as female, many people won't find it unusual for you to try on a men's dress shirt. But, if you were born male and want to try on makeup, you might get a different reaction. No matter who you are, you can find a way that is safe for you. For example, one person we know had his sister take him to buy makeup and clothes, someone else decided to start by wearing women's clothes under his men's clothes, another person only experimented in the privacy of his room until he told his parents, and another switched to men's clothes and told people she was a lesbian until she was ready to tell them that she identified as genderqueer.

And since no one looks the same every day, you get a lot of chances to experiment!

Try It Out!: planning your first experiment

First, write down a few things on the list that follows that someone might do to experiment with gender. Put them in order, from very easy and safe, to things that might really scare you. For example, some people have written the following things: use girls' shampoo, wear men's cologne, wear nail polish, wear jewelry, wear a tie, wear a skirt, wear a bra with stuffing, wear boys' underwear, bind my breasts, stuff my pants, use mascara to paint on sideburns, cut my hair. Feel free to use some of these as well as to come up with some of your own.

NOTE: You do *not* need to do any experiments at all. We just want you to see the possibilities and where they fall on the scale for you. You get to decide what is right for you when.

Scary Scale	Thing I Could Possibly Do
1 (This would be easy.)	
2	
3	
4	
5 (Pretty scary but I'd do it.)	
6	
7	
8	
9	
10 (TOTALLY TERRIFYING!)	

Now pick one thing that falls between 1 and 4 on the scale.

For this thing, answer the questions on the left by filling in the column on the right.

Question	Example Answer	Example Answer	Your Answer
What would your experiment be?	Wear a men's shirt and style my hair in a more masculine way	Put on makeup	
Where would you do this?	With my friend who already knows about this, at their house	My room when my parents are out	
What materials or information (if any) do you need to carry it out?	A men's shirt and a comb	Makeup and some info on how to put it on	
How will you get them?	I already have a comb. I will buy a shirt at the thrift store.	The drug store and the Internet to find out how	
Who would be with you, if anyone?	My friend Jill	No one	
What are some safety factors you need to consider? This is so *you* feel comfortable and so you aren't accidentally outed before you're ready.	Just make sure she knows not to tell anyone, stay in the house, don't take pics	Go to drug store away from school. Don't send pics to anyone. Know how to wash it off!	
How long will you plan to do it?	Just an hour	20 mins to a half hour, depending on how long I have	

In case you want to try some more, today or in the future, we're giving you some extra space. Feel free to make your own sheets as your experiments continue.

Question	Experiment #2	Experiment #3	Experiment #4
What would your experiment be?			
Where would you do this?			
What materials or information (if any) do you need to carry it out?			
How will you get them?			
Who would be with you, if anyone?			
What are some safety factors you need to consider? This is so *you* feel comfortable and so you aren't accidentally outed before you're ready.			
How long will you plan to do it?			

before jumping in the pool

Before we go any further into actually doing any gender experiments, we want you to think about swimming. Why swimming?!

Well, think about times you've gone swimming. In that moment right before you get in the pool where you have to decide whether or not you even want to, what might you think about? How cold the water is? How hot or chilly you are?

And, now, think about *how* you get in. Are you a "cannonball off the diving board" person? Or a "take an hour to wade in" person? One thing is probably true: you stick your hand or toes in first, to see what you're getting yourself into.

We want you to think of getting started in your gender experiment as "getting in the water."

Try It Out!: testing the water

Think about the first gender experiment you just picked.

How much do you want to "jump in" right away?

1 ——————————————— 5 ——————————————— 10

Not much, I'd actually
like to wait awhile

I can't wait one
more second!

What makes you want to "jump in" quickly?

_____

_____

_____

What makes you want to "wade in" or even stay out of the water for now?

_____

_____

_____

What's the water "like"? How inviting or unfriendly would your family, friends, school, or workplace be for your experiment?

1 ————————————————— 5 ————————————————— 10

Very dangerous   No one would care   Inviting!

NOTE: Some folks have supportive waters to dive into, others do not. If you fear that your experiments might bring some bad consequences to you, it is wise to consider this before jumping into a frozen lake. Only you can decide what is safe for you and what is not. If you feel unsure, try to find a supportive adult who can help you figure out how you can continue your gender journey safely.

putting it all together!

Tell us your thoughts on these three factors when it comes to your first experiment: how much you feel like you want to jump in, what makes you think about wading in, and how friendly the water is.

Example: I can't wait to try out wearing makeup. It is a little scary so maybe I just want to try some blush in private. I think my family might be a little freaked out and I'm not ready to tell them. So, I'll keep things private for now until I do some experiments and figure out what I really need.

_____

_____

_____

_____

If you think that the water would be very uninviting for this particular experiment or you say that you really need to go slow and wade in, respect that in yourself! Even if you're feeling really excited to jump in, you can still take your time to plan an experiment that you feel ready to do. If you got here and you don't feel ready for any reason to do what you wrote about above, go back to *Try It Out!:* Planning Your First Experiment and see if there is something else you can choose that is lower on the Scary Scale. Work through the exercises on that page up to here thinking about that experiment and see if you feel ready for the next section.

let's go swimming!

If you've chosen an experiment, decided there is a way you can do it that is safe, and you feel ready, well then, it's time to go ahead and try it!

Try It Out!: **your gender experiment**

First, look back at the plan you made earlier. Is there anything you would like to change about your plan now that you're thinking about actually doing it? If so, that's fine; it is your experiment after all.

Are you ready? Okay, go ahead, we'll wait…

Well, what happened? We're all waiting to hear! How did your experiment go? How did you feel? Were you excited? Anxious? Happy? Was your experiment more good than bad? Or more bad than good?

_____

_____

_____

_____

What did you learn about yourself?

_____

_____

_____

_____

What did you learn about other people?

_____

_____

_____

_____

What worked well?

_____

_____

_____

_____

What do you wish you could have done differently?

_____

_____

_____

_____

What would you want to try next time?

_____

_____

_____

_____

what's next?

You may have learned that something you tried just wasn't for you. You may have learned that you just loved the thing you tried. Most likely, you felt a mix of things. What you do next is up to you. But, we suggest you try a few of these experiments—even if you think it is something you might not like that much! The point is to learn as much as you can about yourself.

As you do your experiments, you may find that you wish to incorporate some of them into your everyday life. This might mean changing your walk, your clothes, the way you talk, or other things. You may choose to start shaving your face more carefully, painting your nails, cutting your hair short, or wearing a tight sports bra or binder to flatten your chest. For many young people, these are satisfying and exciting changes that really represent who they are.

TIP: For folks who decide they would like to present in a different way to their family, or at school or work, new questions can come up about things like asking others to use different pronouns or a different name. If these questions are coming up for you, be sure to read more about these decisions in chapters 3, 4, and 5.

permanent changes

The changes we've been talking about so far are things that you can try and see how you like them. By doing these experiments, you learn about how you react to change and how it feels to present yourself in the world with different gender expressions.

There are also permanent changes to your body that some—but not all—people find are necessary to feeling happy and healthy. These are sometimes called gender-affirming procedures, medical interventions, or "sex change" procedures.

Figuring out if, how, and when to make permanent decisions requires a lot more thought, planning, and time. For example, some things you might consider include:

- How would this change impact my safety?

- Can I afford this change?

- How would this change impact my relationships?

- Is this the best time in my life for this change?

- How would this change impact my mental health?

- Will this change impact my ability to attend school or work?

- How would this change impact my physical health?

These are obviously major choices. Because of that, most people don't make these choices alone or quickly. In fact, in order to get many medical interventions, the old medical guidelines said that you *had* to talk to a psychologist and wait at least a year before going ahead with permanent changes. The guidelines have changed a bit now because these rules didn't fit well for everyone and actually offended or hurt some people. But even though *some* permanent changes can happen now without talking specifically to a psychologist or waiting for exactly one year, we still think it is extremely helpful to talk with people you trust and to take time to think and plan when it comes to making permanent changes.

That said, we think it is your right to have as much information as possible about what all of the options are for changing gender expression. So here are some basics.

for youth before puberty

hormone or puberty "blockers"

Puberty consists of changes in the body that occur between childhood and adulthood. It can be described by stages, called "Tanner Stages." Sometimes doctors prescribe medications to young people that prevent the production of the masculinizing or feminizing hormones that make changes to the body at puberty. For example, a body with ovaries (assigned female at birth) on hormone blockers would not develop breasts or wider hips or have a period. A body with testes (assigned male at birth) on hormone blockers would not develop facial hair, larger muscles, a taller stature, or a deeper voice. These medications are sometimes prescribed to transgender youth to prevent young people who have not yet been through puberty from developing physical changes that don't match their identity.

Hormone or puberty blockers are often prescribed at the very beginning of puberty, or "Tanner Stage II." Puberty blockers are medications that are given either in the muscle, under the skin, or over the course of one or two years with an implant (a small rod put under the skin in the upper arm). They are very expensive and only sometimes covered by insurance.

There are pictures that can help you find where you are in your puberty, if it has already started. Look at the diagrams and see if you can find where your body is. If you are at Tanner Stage II, it is possible that puberty blockers could be prescribed for you by a specialist for transgender youth. If you are already in Tanner Stage IV or V, the puberty blockers won't be able to take away the changes of puberty, but they may still be recommended to prevent further progression of puberty.

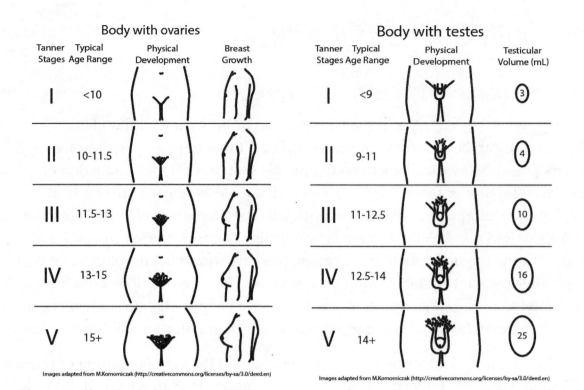

	Body with ovaries					Body with testes		
Tanner Stages	Typical Age Range	Physical Development	Breast Growth		Tanner Stages	Typical Age Range	Physical Development	Testicular Volume (mL)
I	<10				I	<9		3
II	10-11.5				II	9-11		4
III	11.5-13				III	11-12.5		10
IV	13-15				IV	12.5-14		16
V	15+				V	14+		25

Images adapted from M.Komorniczak (http://creativecommons.org/licenses/by-sa/3.0/deed.en)

Images adapted from M.Komorniczak (http://creativecommons.org/licenses/by-sa/3.0/deed.en)

for people after puberty

to appear in a more feminine way:

Hair Removal: Some people who wish to appear more feminine decide to get electrolysis (permanent) or to wax (temporary) to remove facial and body hair. There are not many risks to these procedures and they are not invasive (but can be painful!).

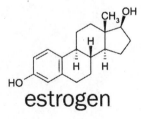

estrogen

Feminizing Hormones: There are several different hormones that when taken together act as "feminizing hormones." They soften skin, redistribute fat, and encourage the growth of breasts. They may also shrink testicles ("balls"), stop body hair growth, and decrease muscle mass. Some people say they experience more mood swings and others do not. These hormones cannot take away facial hair or raise your voice. Some of these changes will go away if you stop hormones, but others, like breast growth, will be permanent. Important: If you take feminizing hormones, you may lose some or all of your fertility. That is, you may become less able to make someone pregnant. However, you should never count on feminizing hormones for birth control, as pregnancies have happened while on hormones.

Genital Surgery: Some people pursue surgeries to make their genitals more feminine. You might have heard of this as a "sex change operation" or "gender reassignment surgery." The surgery to create a vagina is called a vaginoplasty. These surgeries are usually quite successful in changing the appearance in the ways desired. However, any surgery has serious risks. In addition, these surgeries can be expensive and require a long time to recover.

Plastic Surgery: There are a wide variety of other procedures designed to make the face and body appear more feminine, such as breast enlargement or making the "Adam's apple" smaller (called a tracheal shave).

to appear in a more masculine way:

Masculinizing Hormones: The main masculinizing hormone is testosterone (sometimes called "T" or "test"). Those who take it generally become more muscular, grow facial and body hair, and experience a lower voice. They also experience shifts in body fat distribution, an end to menstruation, and clitoral growth (the clitoris, a part of your genitals, gets bigger).

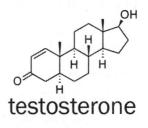

testosterone

Testosterone does not make breasts go away, or cause someone to grow a penis. If you stop taking testosterone, the voice changes, clitoral growth, and facial hair do not go away but other changes may. Important: if you take testosterone, you may lose some of your fertility. That is, you may become less able to get pregnant, but this is not always true. However, you should never count on testosterone for birth control as you *can* get pregnant. Use protection (birth control) if you are sexually active. It is very important to not get pregnant while you are on testosterone, as the testosterone will affect the growing baby. Some transgender males have had healthy pregnancies after stopping testosterone.

Chest Surgery: Some people also pursue surgery to create a more masculine-looking chest. Some people call this "chest reconstruction surgery," "top surgery," or "chest surgery." These surgeries are usually quite successful in changing the appearance in the ways desired. Usually, visible scars from this surgery are permanent. This procedure can also be expensive and take a long time to recover from.

Genital Surgery: Some also decide to have surgery to make their genitals appear more masculine. This might be called "bottom surgery" or "genital reconstruction surgery." There are a variety of procedures that can be pursued, with different changes in appearance and side effects for each. No current surgeries can create something that looks and functions fully like a penis, but some surgeries can elongate the genitals to look more like a penis, and/or create a way for someone to pee standing up. As we said above, any surgery has serious risks. In addition, these procedures can be extremely expensive and take a long time to recover from.

for anyone considering medical interventions

Because these "medical interventions" are what gets talked about the most, many young people who discover that their gender is different from their peers' believe that this is their only option. We disagree. There are many young people we've worked with who have discovered that their gender identity and expression is perfect without any medical intervention at all! Hormones or other interventions do not make you any more of a "real" man or woman. Listen to these people's stories:

Lucia is eighteen and grew up as a girl. When she got to college, she discovered that her preferred gender expression was really masculine. She began to talk to other people who felt the same way, and were changing their pronouns and taking hormones. She thought this was what she'd need to do too until she met a woman who identified as a "stud" on her rugby team. She realized that being sporty, wearing masculine clothes, and dating women didn't mean she needed hormones or surgeries to be able to be herself. She continues to dress in a more masculine way.

Jake also grew up as a girl, but always felt like a "tomboy." Then one day Jake discovered what it meant to be transgender. After going through a lot of experimentation, and talking with a therapist and his family, Jake changed his name and gender on his driver's license. At first he thought he might want to take testosterone for bigger muscles, but he is a singer so he didn't want his voice to change. He wasn't sure he wanted facial hair either. He thinks he might want top surgery one day but can't afford it now, so instead he wears sports bras to make his breasts appear small. Most of his friends are able to accept him as a male and this feels good to him.

Other people do find hormones or surgery necessary to feel comfortable. For these people, figuring out what interventions to have, when to have them, and how to get them are still big decisions. Each intervention carries its own unique set of considerations, including costs, risks, outcomes, recovery time, the availability of surgeons or other providers, and so on. Also, the interventions that are available are changing rapidly as doctors find new ways of working with transgender people and transgender youth in particular. Therefore, we strongly encourage anyone considering medical interventions to carefully research all of the updated options available, talk to medical doctors and surgeons who are experienced at providing those interventions, and talk to therapists who have experience working with transgender people if they need support while sorting it all out.

Try It Out!: your body, your gender

That was a lot of information to take in about what permanent changes are possible when it comes to gender expression! Many people aren't sure what would fit for them when faced with all of the options. So let's do some more Gender Questing!

Imagine yourself in your ideal dream body. What would this body look like? Either draw a picture or create a collage here. (For a collage you can cut out images from magazines, or newspapers, or use images you print from online.)
Is your body today different from your dream body? We bet you said yes. How did we know? Is it because you are reading this book? Nope! It's actually because just about everyone in the whole world wishes they could change their body in some way. Some people want to change their weight, their height, the size of their nose, the color of their skin, the type of hair they have, how hairy they are, how straight their teeth are…and on and on.

Some of these things relate to gender and some of these things do not. Some of these things are permanent changes and some of these things are not. Some of these things are possible and some, unfortunately, are not.

Look back at your picture. In what ways would your body have to change to be like this dream body?

_____

_____

_____

_____

What feelings come up when you look at this list?

_____

_____

_____

_____

Sometimes it can feel good to dream about changes. But sometimes, when changes seem out of reach, or are for sure impossible, it can be quite sad, frustrating, discouraging, or other not very pleasant emotions. In moments when you feel those things, remember that you are not alone. All of us authors have had those feelings about our bodies. We are happy and healthy people today despite those feelings. We know you can be too.

Now for the next step: If you wrote any things down that are permanent changes related to your gender expression, circle them. Maybe you don't even need to move your pen—there are no circles at all. Maybe you just ran out of ink circling everything.

If you did end up circling some things, keep reading this chapter. If you didn't circle anything, you can read the rest of this chapter if you're curious, but you might also decide to move on to chapter 3.

what to do if you are considering permanent changes

So here it is: What if you decide you want to make some permanent changes?

Well, a big question requires a pretty long answer. So here we go:

First, we strongly recommend that anyone considering medical interventions speak with a medical provider who has worked with other transgender and gender expansive youth. They can provide you with up-to-date, reliable medical information about what interventions are available for you specifically (and this is information you can't actually get online). If you don't know of someone in your area, and don't know where to start looking, check out the online list of resources.

We also suggest that if at all possible, you work with a therapist trained in working with transgender and gender expansive youth. These folks can be very helpful as you fully explore pros and cons, the risks and benefits of the different options. They can also help you access medical interventions that you might not otherwise be able to get. Again, if you don't know of a therapist in your area, and don't know where to start looking, check out the list of resources available at the website for this book.

Finally, we think it's wise to do some of your own information gathering on the options that interest you. You can gather information in many places; the most common are websites, books, films, and asking other transgender people. *BUT* (yes, that's a big "but"), as you do this, we want you to keep in mind the following:

- There are many myths and rumors about what hormones and surgeries can and cannot do! Or in other words, a lot of people believe things are true that just are not.

- Everyone has a different experience.

- People may encourage or even pressure you about starting hormones or getting surgery. They may have good intentions, but the last thing you need is to make a decision based on what someone else wants for you! After all, you are the one who has to live in your body for the rest of your life, not them.

- There may be people who try to cheat or scam you. For example, they may say that you can achieve results using some herb or supplement they are promoting without needing a doctor's prescription. If you fall for these scams you can lose not only your money, but your health.

- Some people will tell you they can get you hormones without a prescription. As tempting as it may be, *do not do this*. Hormones are complicated, powerful things. Regular visits with a medical provider are important to make sure that your dose is correct. Hormones have side effects and impacts on the body that may be dangerous for people with certain conditions. Also, just like the herbs and supplements above, hormones purchased online may be dangerously contaminated with other chemicals, or may not even contain the hormone you want.

final note

When it comes to permanent changes like hormones or surgeries, many doctors, therapists, and parents want young people to wait until they are at least eighteen to decide what they want. For those who really need these changes, it can feel overwhelming and cruel to wait!

If you are one of these people who feel like you are pulling your hair out waiting, here are some things you might consider.

- Some doctors are willing to work with youth on obtaining medical interventions earlier. However, this is usually still only an option for young people who have supportive parents and the finances or insurance to afford treatment.

- You are not alone in waiting. Like we said above, most transgender people have had to wait a long time before making permanent changes. It is actually only recently that things are starting to change for the better. So use the skills in chapter 8 to stay strong and make it through the difficult waiting period.

- Find support. The process can be easier to cope with if you know others that are going through the same thing. Seek out local or online support groups.

- In the meantime, you can do some planning about how you will reach your goals eventually. For example, some people make a budget to figure out how to save for a surgery, while other people do research on the different options so they know they will be ready when the time comes.

- As you wait, better interventions may be developing. Over the years, surgery techniques have improved and more information has become available on hormones and transition. You may have a better experience as a result of letting a little time pass.

- Finally, no matter what happens to your body, it doesn't take away anything from who you truly are on the inside. Your gender identity is yours, no matter what other people see or say.

summary

After reviewing this chapter you may decide that you want to do a lot more gender experimenting. We encourage you to do so! You can do this at a pace that you think is right for you. You can even keep a journal of gender experiments. For each one, you can create a plan using the questions in *Try It Out!:* Planning Your First Experiment, *Try It Out!:* Testing the Water, and *Try It Out!:* Your Gender Experiment.

If you found out that you might also want to make some permanent changes, we can't emphasize enough how important it is to find a medical provider and therapist who can help you in achieving your goals.

chapter 3

family

Having explored your gender identity and expression a bit more, you get that while gender is a personal thing, it also influences your interpersonal relationships.

Often some of the most lasting and important relationships we have (for good or for bad!) are with our family members. When we say family member, we usually mean

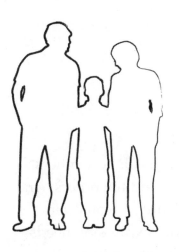

parents, caregivers, siblings, and other relatives. Ideally these people love and support us no matter what gender identity or expression we have. But just like gender is more complicated than its standard definition, relationships with family members are more complicated than images you see with all family members happy and holding hands. (Who would really want to walk around like that all the time anyway?!)

All people usually find that their families are more supportive of some parts of who they are and how they express themselves than other parts. For example, someone we know feels like she is much louder and more extroverted than her family members, and that she doesn't quite fit in her family in this way. Another person is not allowed to bring his boyfriend to his house because his parents don't like that he is dating another boy.

Depending on how your gender identity and expression fits with your family members' ideas about gender, you may be wondering: *So...do I have to talk to my family about this stuff?* or *Is it even possible to get my family member to understand my gender?*

Quick answers:

No, you don't have to tell anyone anything. The important thing is that you make the best decision for yourself. Some people choose to come out and tell their families everything about their sense of gender. Others decide the timing isn't right, or that they only want to discuss some things with certain family members, or that their gender experiences will be something that they don't share at all with family. In this chapter, we'll talk about how to make these decisions and how to have conversations if you'd like.

Yes, it is possible to help family members better understand your gender. Unfortunately, this doesn't mean you have a lot of control over their thoughts or feelings. (We're still working on a machine for that!) But it does mean that there are some resources and strategies that can be helpful. So we'll also talk more about this later in the chapter.

sharing your gender with family members

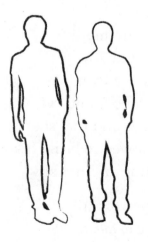

When a person's gender identity does not match how others see them, some people choose to come out and tell others. And even when a person feels their gender identity is consistent with how others see them, but their gender expression needs to change, this can bring up pressure to come out and talk to others. Having these conversations with family members can be one of the scariest parts of exploring gender. Actually, thinking about doing it is usually the scariest. It's kind of like a roller coaster in that way—just before it starts down that first hill is when people are most afraid.

What do people worry about before the coming out roller coaster takes its plunge? They may fear being rejected, being beaten up, losing relationships, losing respect, being kicked out of their house, being laughed at, or being told they are crazy. These fears make sense because some transgender and gender expansive people do experience these things. However, many do not. Often, coming out means there are some adjustments and changes in family relationships, but not a total loss of relationships. In fact, the relationship changes that take place can sometimes be positive, and increase how honest and close a person feels in their family relationships.

So with all of these possible reactions, how can anyone know how their family would react?

family openness

Amina has recently figured out that what has been making her feel different all of these years is that she is actually transgender. She wants to socially transition to female, but her family doesn't know what is going on with her. They think she is just depressed and they still think of her as Rasheed. Amina remembers getting in trouble when she was young for trying on her mom's clothes and high heels. Her parents explained to her very clearly that boys don't do that and that it's not normal. Since then, Amina has hidden all of her feminine feelings and expressions from her parents. Even though a lot of time has passed, Amina remembers her parents' reaction and worries that their reaction to her news of being transgender will be even worse.

Each family has different beliefs, values, and feelings that influence how openly they might react to learning more about your gender identity and expression. Let's take some time to look at how open your family may be. Keep in mind that, even if you don't feel like your family is very open right now, this

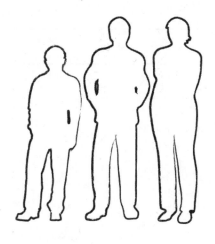

can change over time. Just like most of us needed time to learn about and adjust to the idea of different gender identities and expressions, and just like we had a lot of thoughts, questions, and complicated feelings as we explored gender, many families need time to learn and adjust as well.

Try It Out!: family attitudes

Take some time to think about and answer these questions:

First, who would you consider your immediate family?

_____

_____

_____

Even in one family, different people can have really different feelings and attitudes about things. Let's look at your different family members' feelings or attitudes around areas of diversity in general, such as race, religion, ability, and social class. For each family member you named above, write down how you think they react to issues of diversity in some or all of these areas.

_____

_____

_____

_____

_____

_____

What messages have you have received from these different family members about LGBT people?

_____

_____

_____

_____

_____

What messages have you received from each family member about transgender or gender expansive people in particular?

_____

_____

_____

_____

_____

Oftentimes different family members have different levels of knowledge about gender diversity. For each immediate family member, write what you think their level of knowledge is.

_____

_____

_____

_____

_____

_____

Just like we each face outside pressures to think and act certain ways regarding gender, so did each of your family members! As you can imagine (since you've probably experienced this yourself), a family member could even be pulled in different directions by these different influences.

The mom of a seventeen-year-old just learned that her daughter feels like a boy and identifies as transgender. She is confused by all of the different feelings she is experiencing. This mom is a liberal Democrat, African American, and the daughter of a Baptist minister. The liberal part of her believes in equality for all and feels like she should be able to easily accept her child for who she (or he) is. The part of her who was raised by her Baptist minister father questions whether being transgender is really right and believes that God doesn't make mistakes. She also worries about how her African American friends and community will look at her differently if they find out. She loves her child and at the same time wonders if she will be able to accept this.

For each person you named in your family, write about the different forces that might shape their attitudes about gender diversity:

_____

_____

_____

_____

_____

_____

_____

_____

Your answers to these questions may help you understand how open your family members are to gender diversity. For most people, family members' attitudes are not completely negative or completely positive, but fall somewhere in between.

The thing about attitudes, beliefs, and knowledge is that they all change over time. In fact, research shows us we all change our minds a lot more than we think. For instance, I bet you know someone (surely not yourself!) who has been head over heels in love with someone one week and then the next week, they are...well...over it. Well, that's how it goes with our thoughts and feelings. They change way more than we expect them to.

This is usually a good thing when it comes to family attitudes about gender diversity. For many people, the openness of family members gets more positive over time. Sometimes the progress goes in a jagged line—two steps forward, one step back, and so on. Sometimes the progress goes painfully slowly. Sometimes people can change attitudes pretty quickly. It all depends on a lot of factors, including those influences you wrote about above.

conversations with family members

First things first. If you feel that you may not be safe in your home as a result of sharing more about your gender with your family, you probably want to hit the pause button and do some thinking, planning, and talking with any trustworthy adults you can find. For example, sometimes coming out right away is just not an option (like if you are likely to face violence, homelessness, or other serious dangers as a result). Therefore, some people decide to wait until they are older and have more independence before coming out to their family. Others are able to make some plans with those trusted adults that they've talked with so that they can come out while knowing they will be safe. It is up to you to decide how and when it is wise to have any conversations about your gender with your family members.

If you've decided that talking to your family members is something you'd like to consider further, you might not be sure where to start. For example, coming out is a process that involves talking with many different people in your life. With all of these conversations, you might wonder: *Can't I just get a big loudspeaker and say it to everyone at once?!* But actually, it may be helpful to think about the different considerations for telling each person in your family.

> *Saanvi has thought long and hard about how and if she should tell her family about her gender identity. She worries that her dad will be especially angry because he doesn't seem to have positive feelings about LGBT people. On the other hand, Saanvi wonders if she and her dad may be able to bond more if she is being honest about her feelings. Besides, Saanvi thinks that even if her dad is angry, once her dad talks to her mom, he will probably just go with what her mom says. That's what happened when Saanvi's cousin came out as gay. Saanvi's dad first reacted negatively, but after talking with Saanvi's mom, he has just stayed quiet. And Saanvi's mom is supporting her cousin…so Saanvi wonders if maybe she should talk to her mom first?*

Try It Out!: who do I talk to first?

Here are some of the questions you may ask yourself:

Are there family members you believe to be most likely to understand what you want to tell them about your gender?

_____

Are certain family members more likely to tell other family members you aren't ready to tell?

_____

Are there certain family members that you want to tell soon? Why?

_____

_____

Are there certain family members you are definitely not ready to tell? Why?

_____

_____

After those questions, you may have some ideas about where to start. Keep in mind that there is no one right way to talk to your family members. For example, it is okay for you to tell one person at a time, or to tell everyone at one time. You should decide what is right for you based on what you think will be the best for you and your relationships.

Try It Out!: preparing to talk to your family member about your gender

For each family member who you wish to talk to, answer the following questions:

What exactly would you want to have this person understand about you and your gender identity and expression?

_____

_____

_____

What words, language, and approach do you think will be best to get this person to understand this message?

_____

_____

It helps if you can anticipate concerns or questions the person may have. What do you think they might worry about or be confused about?

_____

_____

_____

What things can you communicate to your family member to address the concerns or confusions you named above?

_____

_____

_____

In talking to this family member, what would be the best-case scenario?

_____

_____

_____

In talking to this family member, what would be the worst-case scenario?

_____

_____

_____

When having conversations to help family members better understand your gender, you may feel that you need to say everything perfectly. That is simply too much pressure for one conversation. Remember, if they ask questions you don't know the answer to, or respond in a way that feels bad, or if you don't get across what you want them to understand, that's okay. Just because you've bravely gone on a

Gender Quest doesn't mean you need to be the Gender Professor for everyone! You can always say you want to pause the conversation and talk about it more another time. In the meantime, it may be a good idea to tell your family members about any resources where they can learn more themselves (look in the list of resources at the website for this book). And then give yourself a pat on the back for being brave enough to try to talk with them.

bumps in the road toward acceptance

Oftentimes, people who are getting ready to talk to their families about their gender imagine only the worst-case scenarios, like being rejected, being kicked out of the house, or being told they are sick or crazy. But these conversations are often not as big of a disaster as is imagined; some even go really well. Therefore, we recommend that you, as the saying goes, "expect the best and plan for the worst." Let's think about the potential difficult things that might come up so you can get through any rough spots more smoothly.

Try It Out!: **seeing into the future**

For each of the worst-case scenarios you named above, list the supports you could use if needed (such as friends, LGBTQ people in person or online, staff at your school, or a therapist):

_____

_____

_____

In these scenarios, what are things you could do to keep yourself both emotionally and physically safe (such as disclose your gender identity in a letter or in a public place, or identify a place you can go after the disclosure)?

_____

_____

_____

How much do you rely on your family for your physical needs—food, a place to live, and so on? If there is any risk you might not get these things from your family for a while, who else might be able to provide support?

_____

_____

_____

How much do you rely on your family for your emotional needs—feeling self-confident and hopeful? If some members of your family are struggling to accept your gender identity, whom could you turn to for support?

_____

_____

_____

Is there any chance that you might not be physically safe after talking to your family? If so, what plans might you make or supports might you turn to in order to stay safe?

_____

_____

_____

For many people, family is whom we rely on. Since family members may take time to adjust and understand what you are telling them, it is helpful to make sure you have other supports first. Then even if your family is totally accepting, outside support is just a great bonus!

What can you do and whom can you turn to if difficult challenges arise?

_____

_____

_____

Talking to family members about your gender is an act that requires a lot of energy and courage. This deserves to be celebrated! List some ways in which you can celebrate after your conversations, no matter how they go:

_____

_____

_____

_____

Finally, remind yourself that your family members have experienced the same rigid rules around gender as you did before your Gender Quest. Therefore, they most likely will need their own time to understand and accept your gender if it doesn't fit into their current understanding. Your family members' initial reactions probably won't represent their attitudes and beliefs over time.

That said, as understanding as you are about your family's need for time, it of course won't stop any negative words and actions from being hurtful! In many instances, with support from other people in your life and some strong coping skills (like those in chapter 8, Dealing with the Hard Stuff), people can keep themselves doing okay even when their family is in the early stages of adjusting. There are some times though when being patient with family isn't the right choice. Hopefully this isn't true for you, but if you are experiencing violence at home, it's time to do something! Speak to a teacher, school counselor, therapist, doctor, or police officer about what's happening—they can help you figure out how to get to a safer situation.

expressing what you need in family relationships

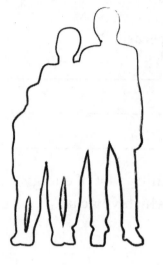

Aiden cringes as his mom calls him down for dinner by saying, "Nicole, come downstairs!" Aiden has told his mom about his feelings about his gender, knowing that even though he was born with what people think of as a girl's body, he really is a boy. His mom has noticed his masculine clothing and regularly encourages Aiden to dress in a more feminine way. Every time Aiden's mom comments on his clothing, uses his given female name or pronouns, or emphasizes what a "pretty girl" he is, Aiden feels like screaming! He wishes that his mom could see who he really is and love him as her son, rather than her daughter.

Like we've been saying, family members often need their own time to learn and adjust to new ways of thinking about your gender. While your family members need their own space in doing that, your feelings are important too!

Try It Out!: **what do you need?**

What do you need from your family members during periods of adjustment to feel safe and valued?

_____

_____

_____

Sometimes when people talk about gender diversity, family members are able to accept the "idea," but struggle with doing things differently, like using a different name, switching between "he" and "she," or not reacting in negative ways to changes in dress or hair. Your family may do or say things during this time that are hurtful to you without wanting to do this or even realizing that they have. It may be helpful for you to talk with your family about the effect their actions are having on you. For example, if you can talk to them about how it feels each time they use your birth name or pronouns, they may be more likely to put effort into changing. If you find that these types of conversations do not seem to go well, family therapy may be a helpful option for you. If possible, find a therapist who has experience working with transgender and gender expansive people so they can be most helpful to you and your family. (See chapter 8, Dealing with the Hard Stuff, for tips about finding a therapist.)

summary

Both preparing for and actually talking to your family about your gender can be daunting, exciting, stressful, wonderful, difficult, powerful, exhausting, a huge relief—and possibly all of these at the same time. Whether or not you are thinking about talking or taking steps toward it, be sure to give yourself credit for all the energy and courage you are showing! And finally, remember to use the supportive people you have in your life wherever you can find them—in your family or outside!

chapter 4

school and work

When your gender doesn't fit other people's expectations, it can sometimes bring up challenges at school or work. For example, some people who express gender differently have faced bullying or discrimination in these settings. As you figure out how you wish to express gender at your school or at work, let's discuss some tips that may be helpful in overcoming any challenges that arise.

advocating for yourself

In the past year, Aaliyah came out to her foster parents as transgender and is beginning her social transition to female. She is starting high school in a couple months and wants to start in her new school as a girl. Her foster parents know about this, and are okay with it, but they are still having a hard time fully accepting Aaliyah's female identity, still sometimes calling her by her birth name. Aaliyah wonders about how to handle the school situation and doesn't feel like her foster parents are ready to help her with it. She has tons of questions and is not sure where to start. Will the teachers be able to call her Aaliyah? Will she be bullied? What bathroom should she use? Whom should she talk to about all this?

While many people worry about being accepted at school or work, not everyone has problems. Nevertheless, it can be good to know how to advocate for yourself.

As unfair as it is, the truth is that young people and people of marginalized groups (such as racial minorities or people with disabilities, as well as transgender and gender expansive people) have extra hurdles to overcome when having their voice heard. First, it can be harder to speak up for yourself if you haven't had many opportunities in the past to be empowered and use your voice. Second, it can be harder to get the people around you who are in power (such as school or college administrators, or bosses at work) to listen and respect your perspective when you are young or of a minority status.

Therefore, when advocating for yourself, it can be very helpful to have others, either a group of peers or other adults, who are able to support you in communicating. Having these other people saying what you're saying acts almost like a microphone—making your voice louder so more people can hear it.

middle, junior, and high school

Some youth find that parents and caregivers are best able to help them communicate to other adults at school. If parents and caregivers are supportive of your needs and can echo what you are saying to the teachers and administrators at school, your voice is more likely to be heard. Other young people find it too hard to speak to their parents, or find that their parents or caregivers aren't able to support them in this

way. If this is the case, don't fret! There are some other ways to get your voice heard.

For young people, if you do find that you need extra support from outside your family, one place to start is to find out if your school has a Gay-Straight Alliance (GSA) or some other organization that is supportive to gay, lesbian, bisexual, or transgender students. If your school does have a GSA, consider joining it. There, you can get support from other students like you, and possibly connect with the teacher who facilitates the group. This person can be an important source of support and information at your school. If your school does not have a GSA, it may be helpful to find a supportive teacher or school counselor who can understand your perspective. Keep your eyes peeled and your ears open for any signs that a teacher or school counselor may be gender-friendly, such as a safe zone sticker or discussion of sexual orientation or gender identity in class. If you are unable to find a person to help you advocate inside the school, you can also look for a supportive therapist

SAFE ZONE

or organization outside of the school system. You can search online for therapists and LGBTQ youth centers in your area to see if you can connect with someone who understands your needs.

college

For people in college, similar resources may exist to connect with peers who support you in advocating for yourself, such as campus LGBTQ groups. In addition, it may be helpful to make contact with the Student Support Services on the campus you have chosen. You can do so even before you actually arrive on campus if you like. Representatives in these offices are there to help all students with personal and unique needs. Student support staff can help you think about the specific gender-related challenges you may face on their campus and also what resources may be available to help you with your adjustment to college. They may be able to suggest ways for you to connect with other transgender, gender expansive, or LGBTQ students, which could give you a sense of community at the school.

at work

Similarly, finding the appropriate person or people to help you advocate for yourself at work can be very helpful. In work settings, supervisors and Human Resources personnel set the tone and expectations for how employees are treated. For this reason, it can be helpful to discuss your needs or concerns with your supervisors. If your supervisor is unable or unwilling to assist you, speak to the people in Human Resources. While you may need to do some work to educate your supervisor or Human Resources personnel about transgender issues first, getting their backing can be a huge advantage. When a workplace takes an official stance, other employees will often fall in line.

However, we shouldn't ignore the powerful role that workers can have when they speak together. Some large organizations have LGBTQ groups. If yours does, this can be a fantastic resource. If not, consider whether you have any potential allies among your coworkers. Also consider speaking with people in LGBTQ groups at outside organizations to see how things are handled in other workplaces.

Try It Out!: my advocacy supports

Who are the possible people in leadership at your school or workplace that might be able and willing to help you navigate any issues related to gender in your school or work settings?

_____

_____

Who are the people outside your school or workplace that might assist you in advocating for yourself?

_____

_____

Are there peers at school or work who could be helpful in your efforts?

_____

_____

Once you identify who might be helpful to you in advocating for yourself, you have to communicate with them about what is going on and what you need or want from them. Depending on whom you are asking, this might be super easy, or very difficult, or somewhere in between. However, it is always helpful to have a good idea of what you want to communicate. In the following spaces, write each potential supporter's name. Then consider what will be important for you to tell them by answering the questions under their names. (Feel free to do this for more than three people even though we only have three spaces here.)

Name: _____

What do you want to make sure they know about what has been going on for you?

_____

_____

What do you want or need for them to do to help? (If you aren't sure what would help yet, sometimes what you need is for them to just help you brainstorm what you and they can do together.)

_____

_____

Name: _____

What do you want to make sure they know about what has been going on for you?

_____

_____

What do you want or need for them to do to help?

_____

_____

Name: _____

What do you want to make sure they know about what has been going on for you?

_____

_____

What do you want or need for them to do to help?

_____

_____

Here are some tips for getting ready to advocate for yourself:

- *Do your homework:* First, educate yourself on the laws and policies in your state, town, and school or workplace. Seek information from organizations that provide help to transgender and LGBT individuals at work and school (see the online list of resources for suggestions). These organizations can give you further tips on and information about your rights. Also try to find out what other students or employees have done in your situation. We highly recommend the resources at the Gay-Straight Alliance Network website.

- *Check in with your emotions:* You might feel defensive, angry, or scared when you have to talk to someone who may or may not really understand your needs. However, your approach can make a big difference. As much as possible, be respectful, calm, and clear about what you need.

- *Get specific:* It is important to know what you're asking for when you speak to someone who can help. That is, if you want to be able to use a certain bathroom, give your reasons for this and offer information about how this has worked for other students or employees in your situation. If you want your school or workplace to take a stand on bullying or harassment, point out the impact it's had on your life, and show how school or work policies support your request.

- *Offer information:* Many people are uninformed about transgender issues. You might consider offering books, websites, or other information to those who wish to help but aren't sure how. (See the online resource list for suggestions.)

- *Keep your cool:* Even well-meaning people might slip up and use the wrong pronoun, ask questions that you consider offensive, or simply be ignorant. Try to keep your eyes on the goal—getting assistance with what you need.

Now hopefully you have some ideas about who can assist you with any challenges you face at school or work, and how you can go about getting this support. Remember, you are not alone in this journey.

Now let's address some of the more common challenges gender expansive and transgender people have faced at school or work and see what others have done or found helpful.

name and pronouns

When your gender doesn't line up with the box the doctor checked for you at birth, the name and pronouns (such as he/him and she/her) that you were assigned or given may not match the way you feel on the inside. Many gender expansive and transgender people choose names and pronouns for themselves that are a better fit. (Later in this section you'll find a chart with some different options for pronouns you might choose.) It is sometimes difficult at first for other people to switch and use different pronouns or names if they've used other terms before, or to call us by something that doesn't seem to fit with their binary understanding of gender. But you still have the right to ask people to refer to you as you choose, and expect that they will do so, even if it's difficult for them at first.

What name(s) have you considered using during your gender journey?

_____

_____

Which name do you currently prefer to be called?

_____

Have you already asked people at school or work to use this name? If not, how ready do you feel to ask these people to use your chosen name? Circle the response that most closely matches your feelings:

1	2	3	4	5
Not ready at all. I'm not sure if that's the name I will stick with, or I am not that sure if I am ready to ask others to call me by that name.	I have definite hesitations.	Not sure. I have mixed feelings about asking people to use this name.	Almost there!	Totally ready! That is the only name I will answer to.

The chart below shows a few gender-binary and gender-neutral pronoun options.

Gender	Subject	Object	Possessive Adjective	Possessive Pronoun	Reflexive
Binary	She	Her	Her	Hers	Herself
Binary	He	Him	His	His	Himself
Neutral	They	Them	Their	Theirs	Themself
Neutral	Ze	Zir/Hir	Zir/Hir	Zirs/Hirs	Zirself/Hirself
Neutral	E	Em	Eir	Eirs	Emself

What pronoun(s) do you believe fit you best and respect your gender identity?

_____

Have you already asked people at school or work to use these pronouns for you? If not, how do you think they would respond if you asked them to use the pronouns that affirm your gender?

_____

_____

_____

If you are planning to ask others to refer to you by a different name and pronoun than they are used to or than is printed on your legal documents, it may be helpful to refer to the section Advocating for Yourself at the beginning of this chapter. Think about who the people in leadership are in your school or work environment, as well as the other support people you identified. For example, if you believe it could be helpful, you could have a guidance counselor at your school speak to other teachers about how it is appropriate to refer to you in class; or you could have Human Resources personnel at your workplace speak with your boss or any employees who are having difficulty referring to you appropriately at work; or you might speak to the registrar at your college to figure out how to have your chosen name and pronouns listed on transcripts, ID cards, or course rosters.

bathrooms, locker rooms, and uniforms

As Demarco started middle school and as boys and girls seemed to become more and more separated, his feelings of being different from his peers became more difficult for him. He has spent the last several months exploring his gender and has found that he likes a lot of things that are considered feminine, such as makeup and the colors pink and purple. He doesn't feel like he is a girl, but that he just wants to be free to be whomever he is, whether that is masculine or feminine, and however that might differ from day to day. Since he has

started to express a wider range of gender, he has felt more and more uncomfortable being grouped with the boys in school, especially in the bathrooms and locker rooms where he sometimes worries about getting bullied.

When your gender assigned at birth does not match with how you feel on the inside, it is often uncomfortable and upsetting to be forced into spaces and behaviors that ignore your gender identity. This can happen when it comes to bathrooms, locker rooms, and uniforms. For example, think about a student who was assigned a female gender at birth but identifies as a boy and has a very masculine gender expression. When this boy is forced to wear female uniforms, forced to use the female bathrooms, and to change in the female locker rooms, it can be really uncomfortable for him. Some schools and states have policies or laws that say that transgender and gender expansive youth must be able to use facilities in line with their gender identities. Sometimes this means allowing a transgender or gender expansive person to use a gender-neutral bathroom or a nurse's or coach's office to change for gym class. Other times it means allowing a person to use the bathrooms and locker rooms that fit their gender identity. While some schools and workplaces will be very responsive to what you prefer, this isn't true everywhere. If it's not true for you at your school or workplace, you might try using the advocacy skills you learned above to try to get things changed.

Are there things at school that force you into gender spaces and behaviors that are uncomfortable (for example, bathrooms, locker rooms, uniforms, or lining up by boys and girls for recess)?

_____

_____

_____

_____

What feelings do you have when you are in these situations and what do you do about them?

_____

_____

_____

How would you like to see these situations handled (for example, be able to use a different unisex bathroom, be able to use the girls' locker room)?

_____

_____

_____

After what you learned in the Advocating for Yourself section of this chapter, what steps do you think you might try to get things to change as you would like?

_____

_____

_____

_____

harassment and bullying

In eleventh grade, Judith, who used to identify as a lesbian, decided to begin a social transition to male and is now going by the name of Ethan. Ethan always had a pretty masculine gender expression and the girls in school made fun of him ever since he can remember. They used to call him a "dyke" long before he even started to consider whether or not he was a lesbian. Now that Ethan has transitioned to a male gender expression, he notices more harassment from the boys and sometimes feels afraid. One day, between classes, two boys approached Ethan in the hallway, called him a "faggot," and punched him in the stomach. Ever since that day, Ethan worries about getting beaten up even worse and is feeling a lot of anxiety every day in school.

Unfortunately, most people experience some harassment and bullying at some point in their lives. This can be even more common for transgender and gender expansive people. If you are experiencing bullying or harassment at school or work, or are afraid you will experience bullying or harassment, there are steps you can take. You deserve to feel safe in your school and workplace just like everyone else.

Have you experienced, seen, or heard about harassment, name calling, or violence in your school or workplace (to you or to someone else)?

_____

_____

_____

_____

Are there times or situations in which you are most worried about being mistreated? (For example, when you go to the bathroom.)

_____

_____

_____

_____

If you or people you know have been mistreated in the past, do you know what was done about it?

_____

_____

_____

What do you think needs to happen in your school or workplace so that you feel safe and don't have to worry as much about bullying or harassment? (For example, to have a private bathroom.)

_____

_____

_____

_____

After thinking about what would make your school or workplace environment safer, it is again usually helpful to have some supports in advocating for yourself. Whether you talk to a parent, a teacher, a counselor, the principal, your boss, colleagues, or Human Resources staff, it is very important that you communicate your experiences and concerns as well as what you think might be helpful. Take a look back at the Advocating for Yourself section for tips on how to talk with these folks. Finally, it may be helpful to find out about the bullying policy in your school, the harassment policy at your workplace, and any laws that may be on your side.

dealing with ignorance

When advocating for yourself, you will likely run into some people who are awesome supports, and also some people who may ask ignorant questions, make mistakes, or even react negatively to you. You may wish to take a moment to consider how you want to respond to these potential situations.

Here are some options:

- *Having a conversation:* If you believe that the other person is not ill-intentioned, but acting out of ignorance or just not knowing how to act, consider taking a moment to speak to this person. If you are able to ask them to adjust their behavior in an assertive way—one that's not critical, but still clear about your feelings—they may be able to understand and change.

- *Ignoring:* Sometimes the best approach is to ignore a comment, especially if it seems like the person is trying to get a negative reaction from you. If you consistently ignore someone's negative comments, they are more likely to stop because they aren't getting the reaction they want.

- *Gaining allies:* If possible, find supportive classmates or coworkers and stick with those people. Consider discussing any problems with these people. Helpful and supportive peers can go a long way to making school or work more satisfying and fun. They can also help set a tone of respect and acceptance with other people at school or work.

- *Activism:* Many changes have been made in schools and workplaces to make them safer and fairer for transgender and gender-nonconforming people. This has been largely due to the activism of transgender people, including students. Many transgender students have been instrumental in starting Gay-Straight Alliances, and changing school policies and even state law. This can be hard, and comes with risks—but also rewards. If you are the type of person who wants to go the extra mile, you might consider helping your school start a Gay-Straight Alliance or taking part in other activism.

summary

Whether you are exploring a transgender or gender expansive expression at school or at work, you deserve to be treated with dignity and respect. While there can be gender-related challenges in these settings, it is possible to overcome these challenges and find solutions. And sometimes you'll find that not only did you make things better for yourself, but also for any future transgender and gender expansive people who come through your school or workplace. (Yes, we applaud your efforts and potential heroism!) We know communicating about these topics can sometimes be very stressful, though, and can require a lot of patience when things don't change immediately. Remember that finding support and help in getting your needs met can be really important, and don't be afraid to reach out to people near and far who might be able to provide this.

chapter 5

friends and other peers

For better or worse, classmates, coworkers, friends, and acquaintances are a really important part of our lives. They're people we turn to for support, for feedback, for fun, and when we need a shoulder to cry on. On the other hand, these are also the people in our lives that can be annoying (or infuriating!), tease or harass us, and do or say things that result in us feeling badly about ourselves.

At this point in your Gender Quest, you may find yourself wishing to talk to friends about what you're thinking about gender, or wanting to show up to school or work dressing and acting in a way that's more consistent with your identity, but worrying about how these people will react.

should I talk about my gender thoughts and experiences?

As you are going through this quest and thinking a lot about your gender, it would make a lot of sense if you feel you want to talk to someone about your insights, feelings, and experiences— maybe to help you figure out what's going on, or just because you want to be real with the people in your life. It's a totally natural impulse. And whether because we just won an award or we're going through something at home, it's healthy to want to talk to others, get support, and share our excitement and our suffering. In fact, research shows that people who have friends and acquaintances to share experiences with are happier and healthier than those who don't.

But you might also have some good reasons to hesitate. Maybe you know others who have been bullied for acting or appearing or thinking differently, or even just because others *think* they're different. Maybe you yourself have experienced bullying for something related to gender, sexual orientation, or something else entirely. If any of these things are true, you may have found yourself being afraid of showing all parts of yourself to friends, classmates, and coworkers. You might not have faith that these people will be accepting, understanding, and supportive. And it can be challenging to know how to respond to people who might have negative reactions to your gender identity or expression, sexual orientation, or other aspects of yourself.

So, how do you decide when and how and to whom to reveal different parts of yourself?

Well, while the fact is that you can never know exactly how a friend or classmate or coworker will react, there are some things you can consider as you decide what you want to reveal to whom. (In other words, you don't need to come out to everyone about everything.)

am I ready to talk?

Try to set aside pressure you might experience to "come out" or to be vocal about who you are all the time. There can be a lot of talk in the media, movies, and books about how important it is to "come out" or to proclaim your pride and confidence in who you are from every rooftop. But really, most people find it wise to make careful decisions about which parts of themselves they share with which people in their lives. For example, if someone's parents are getting divorced, they may want to talk to some people about that, but not others. That certainly makes sense. Talking to people about your gender is another time where you get to decide with whom, when, and how you want to share something about yourself. Just like we talked about in relation to family members, you don't have to have these conversations until you want to, you feel ready to, and you feel safe to do so.

In fact, it's okay to wait for as long as you want to talk to anyone about your gender. If you think that you may be physically or emotionally hurt in a way you aren't prepared to deal with (or in a serious way that no one would ever be ready to deal with), then this is probably not the time to talk to others.

That said, consider also that any big step brings a little risk, so you have to weigh these risks against the potential benefits. Sometimes sharing your thoughts and feelings about your gender, or simply your gender identity or expression, can be a wonderfully liberating experience that brings you much closer to the people around you. So, if you are wondering if, when, and how you might talk to someone, read on…

where should I start?

We strongly recommend, before you start getting on the loudspeaker at school or work or anything, or even talking to your close friends, that first you get support, if possible, from some outside folks. This could mean people at an LGBTQ support group, people on a hotline you call, people in your family whom you've spoken to, a therapist or counselor, or people in your religious community—just anyone outside of your school or work network who does support and understand your gender.

So how do you find this support? Lots of ways.

Our number one suggestion is to look for LGBTQ youth groups in your area that you can attend in person. (Even if you don't identify with any of those letters, there may be people there who might be able to understand what you're going through.) We think this is the best way to start because these groups are usually good bets for finding safety, some cool new friends, and some really helpful information.

There are also many online groups, websites, apps, and social networking sites that people have gained a lot of support and information from. See the resource list on the website for this book for some suggestions. However, before jumping into the waters online, you should keep in mind several things:

- Facebook and other online social networking is not anonymous and your participation on a page or group may be visible to others.

- What you post online stays forever—this includes pictures and comments. If you don't want a picture or comment spread around, don't share it. Even when you use apps that are supposed to "erase" your photo after a certain amount of time, you may still find that your picture has been spread around.

- People online are not always who they seem. Never give out personal information to anyone online.

- Young people have gotten hurt, and do get hurt, meeting up with people they have met online. You may feel in need of in-person support or a date but your safety needs to be considered. If you do consider meeting up with someone you've met online, we strongly recommend meeting them the first time in a public place or with people you already know around. It is also wise to set up a safety plan with someone you trust, such that they (1) know where you will be and (2) agree to check in on you (perhaps by texting or calling) during the meeting, with the understanding that if you don't respond you might be in trouble and they should call for help.

- Since unlike in-person groups, online groups often don't have any moderators there to make sure that there's a positive atmosphere, sometimes bullying can occur, even in what should be a supportive group. Online bullying can make people feel pretty terrible, so we want you to go into this option cautiously and know to disengage from a group if you experience any negativity or things that make you feel uncomfortable.

who should I talk to?

Although you might think of your very best friend as the person you should talk to first, this isn't necessarily true. Why? Well, depending on what their thoughts are about gender, and how they tend to react to things, they may or may not be the wisest first choice. So it makes sense to actually think through whom you want to talk to.

Try it Out!: who's up first?

Name a few people who you think you might be interested in talking to about your gender:

1. _____

2. _____

3. _____

4. _____

5. _____

Let's get to know these people a bit better. First, let's think about their potential reactions.

Person	How open to gender or sexuality diversity do you think they are?	What makes you think this?
1		
2		
3		
4		
5		

So, reviewing this, which of these people seems like they might be the most supportive?

_____

_____

_____

Now, consider for each of those people how likely they are to keep your privacy, if that's what you want. Think about times when they've kept or told other private information of yours or someone else's. Have they been trustworthy?

Person	How trustworthy are they?	What makes you think this?
1		
2		
3		
4		
5		

Who seems the most trustworthy?

_____

_____

_____

How important are support and privacy to you in this process?

_____

_____

_____

Below, think about how you would feel if the people you chose had the reactions described. How intense would this be for you?

If they were...	I'd feel...
Really excited for me and can't wait to hear all about it	
Happy for me and supportive	
Supportive but don't seem to understand what it means	
Supportive but use the wrong name or pronoun for me, even after I asked them to use my preferred one	
Supportive but have questions that show that maybe they think it is weird	
Not very supportive but seem willing to learn over time	
Not at all supportive but will still be my friend	
Not at all supportive and don't want to be my friend	

How about your privacy? How important is that to you? (Mark anywhere on the line.)

If this happened…	How much of a problem would it be for me?
The person I told hinted a little to a close mutual friend	1 ———————— 5 ———————— 10 Not a problem! I wouldn't like this This would be devastating
The person I talked to told a close mutual friend	1 ———————— 5 ———————— 10 Not a problem! I wouldn't like this This would be devastating
Our conversation got out to our group of friends	1 ———————— 5 ———————— 10 Not a problem! I wouldn't like this This would be devastating
The whole school found out	1 ———————— 5 ———————— 10 Not a problem! I wouldn't like this This would be devastating
My parent/s found out	1 ———————— 5 ———————— 10 Not a problem! I wouldn't like this This would be devastating
My extended family found out	1 ———————— 5 ———————— 10 Not a problem! I wouldn't like this This would be devastating

preparing for different reactions

Something to consider is how you will handle different people's reactions. Hopefully if you do wish to talk to someone, you are choosing a person that you trust will be open and accepting of you! However, as we said, you can never know for sure.

For many relationships, being open and vulnerable about personal things, such as our thoughts and experiences of gender, is really great for the relationship. It encourages trust and understanding, the stuff that healthy, long-lasting relationships are built on. You may feel much closer and appreciative of that relationship, and the person you have spoken to may now be more likely to open up to you about things they hesitated to talk about with others as well.

The fact is, though, that many friends, classmates, or coworkers, even if they are supportive and trustworthy, may not fully understand at first. This is especially true if what you are telling them about your gender is different from how they have been taught to think about gender. So you might need to be prepared for some misunderstandings or confusion, as they go through the stages of their own learning process around gender. Keep in mind that people can and do change over time. In fact, you likely can remember a time when you thought differently about gender. But in the meantime, you might want to be prepared to handle questions or confusions that people have as they try to understand.

For example, some questions that you might get asked are:

Does this mean you are lesbian/gay?

Why can't you just be happy the way you are?

Are you sure?

Are you going to have "the surgery"?

What is "genderqueer"?

How do you know?

Does this mean you're hitting on me?

Did you tell your parents? Are you going to?

Who else knows?

Who can I tell?

Are you changing your name or pronoun?

Can we still be friends?

Isn't that against your religion?

These questions may be coming from a place of caring, concern, or a desire to understand. But they can also feel hurtful to us. This is an example of why we suggest that you have some outside people in your life that can help you deal with any feelings that come up when people ask you such questions.

Oh yeah, and you might be wondering, *So am I supposed to be prepared to answer all of these questions ahead of time?!* And as you might have noticed, no, we aren't suggesting you should figure out how you would respond to every potential question someone might ask, because really, many people will ask questions that will surprise you. What you can do in response to these questions is whatever you need to do to take care of yourself. This means you can try to answer as honestly as possible, or tell people about places they could go to learn more (see Resources for Parents, Family, Friends, and Allies in the online resource list), or even tell them you don't know or that you can't answer that question. After all, just because you know a whole lot about gender now doesn't mean you need to be the Gender Professor (unless, of course, if you want the job!).

dealing with negative experiences

It is possible you have had or will have some negative experiences if you tell people about your gender. Like we've said, many times, friends are simply unsure of how to react and take a little time to adjust. However, some young people experience rejection or bullying as a result of how they look or what they've said.

Here are some other thoughts on dealing with rejection and bullying:

- Turn to those who do support you. If you have friends that are supportive, stick with those people and focus energy on them.

- Reach out in LGBT groups for help and support.

- Get involved with things you love, both in and out of school.

- You may have a lot of strong feelings related to rejection, bullying, or even just misunderstandings. Take the time to talk those feelings through with someone you trust.

- Ask for help from a school counselor or teacher you trust. Some schools have "Safe Zone" posters outside offices of staff who are welcoming of LGBT students.

- Your school should *not* tolerate bullying or harassment of any kind, including that which is based on gender or sexual orientation. If they do, you may need to advocate for yourself and your needs. Try speaking to a counselor, teacher, or administrator (like the principal) whom you trust.

- If you can, talk to your parents.

- Find a therapist you can talk to.

- If you have been physically harmed or assaulted, you have the option of calling 911.

- If you feel really distressed or even suicidal for any reason, call a hotline such as The Trevor Project: 1-866-488-7386, Trans Lifeline: 1-877-565-8860 (US) / 1-877-330-6366 (Canada), or the National Suicide Prevention Lifeline: 1-800-273-8255. See the resource list at the website for this book for more information and websites for chat support.

- If you feel you might hurt yourself or someone else, call 911.

We list other resources related to bullying in the online resource list for this book.

summary

Getting to talk to someone who gets it can be so important. That's why, even though these honest conversations about gender with the people in your life may seem scary or risky, they can also be totally worth it. However, only you can decide who it makes sense for you to tell and when and how you will do this. We highly suggest that, if possible, you access some support outside of the people at school and work, such as by going to a local group or calling one of the hotlines that we list so that you have people to buffer you against any negative reactions. There are thousands of young people just like you out there. If you look, we promise you will find them. Maybe not immediately, but you will. Finally, we are confident that even though it can take some time and patience before you find yourself surrounded by people at work and school who support you, by going through this process you will find some great friends around whom you can feel like your true self. And that is a wonderful thing.

chapter 6

dating and sex

Dating and sex. These are topics that many people have strong or complicated feelings about—some positive, some negative, some neutral or somewhere in between. Some people spend a lot of hours daydreaming or thinking about these topics. Other people couldn't care less about dating or sex. This range of reactions is true for people of all sorts of gender identities and expressions.

 Beginning in adolescence, people usually start figuring out some things about their own sexuality and what types of romantic relationships they want. While romantic and sexual relationships can be exciting, rewarding, and fulfilling, they can also have an impact on our emotional and physical health. Because of the risk of being hurt, it is important to take good care of yourself while exploring romantic and sexual relationships. Making choices that keep you emotionally and physically safe is particularly important when it comes to sexual activity. Examples of ways you can keep yourself safe include only engaging in sexual activity if and when you are feeling mentally ready, and making safer sex choices—including protecting yourself from sexually transmitted infections and unwanted pregnancy.

As you probably already have figured out, gender identity and gender expression influence all sorts of things, and that definitely includes dating and sex. So for people on a Gender Quest, we figured devoting some time to these issues made sense.

In this chapter, we are first going to talk about sexual and romantic orientations, explain what they mean, and give you a chance to think about your own sexual and romantic identities. Then we will dig into the topics of dating and sex. Our aim is to help you get to whatever you envision as being a satisfying relationship with your own sexuality and with any partners in your future.

sexual and romantic orientations

After exploring just how complicated gender identity can be, we're sure you will not be surprised that sexual and romantic orientations are also fairly complicated concepts. Often when we think of sexual orientation we think about someone's sexual attractions and behaviors, and of identifying as asexual, heterosexual, lesbian, gay, bisexual, or pansexual. Similarly, some people distinguish between romantic orientation—"romantic orientation" meaning whom someone is emotionally attracted to and engaged with. They may identify as aromantic, biromantic, and so on. But what does any of that really mean? And how do we know what we are?

sexual orientation

Sexual orientation can actually be separated into (at least) three parts: attractions, behaviors, and identity.

Sexual attractions indicate whom we want to be close to physically. You might have fantasies about kissing someone, urges to touch that person, or a desire to have sex with them. These are indicators of sexual attraction.

Behaviors are the actions we take that could be seen if someone was watching us. Sexual behaviors could mean all sorts of things including searching on the Internet for pictures of someone you think is pretty, masturbating (touching yourself in sexual ways), flirting, or being physically intimate with another person.

Identity is a little more complicated—it is how we label ourselves. Often our sexual identities match up with our attractions, and sometimes with our sexual behaviors too. However, it is common for not all behaviors to match up perfectly with our identities.

Attractions, behaviors, and identity usually go together to some degree. But despite what most people think, there usually isn't a perfect alignment between these things. Some common examples of sexual identities and their definitions are below:

Lesbian: A woman who is attracted to women

Gay: Most often, a man who is attracted to men, though sometimes also used by women who are attracted to women

Bisexual: A person who is attracted to men and women

Heterosexual: A person who is attracted to the "opposite" sex

Pansexual: A person who is attracted to people of all sorts of sexes and genders

Asexual: Someone who is not interested in sex or is not sexually attracted to others

Queer: A person who has a non-heterosexual identity

However, these labels aren't fixed or absolute; they don't always match perfectly with behaviors or attractions. For example, there are many women who identify as lesbians but have had sex with more men than women and have been in love with a man. There are also many men who are attracted to other men and are comfortable talking about the fact that they have had sex with other men, but do not identify with the terms "gay" or "bisexual." As another example, there are plenty of men who are attracted to men but feel uncomfortable or unsafe acting on these attractions or defining themselves as gay.

As you can see, while these three things—attraction, behavior, and identity—are related, they don't necessarily need to align exactly. In fact, it is totally fine and normal for there to be differences between your attractions, your behavior, and your identity.

romantic orientation

Similarly, romantic orientation can be divided into attraction, behavior, and identity. Your romantic attraction reflects whom you are drawn to be close to emotionally. For example, when you are romantically attracted to a person, you may find yourself wanting to develop a close special connection with them, where you tell them your thoughts and feelings and hear about theirs, where you support each other through hard times and celebrate with each other in good times, where you do special things for each other and spend special one-on-one time together.

Your romantic behavior consists of the many types of things you do with your romantic partner(s) to be emotionally close. For example, you might go out on dates with your romantic partner, buy them gifts, write them love notes, make them a playlist of love songs, confide in them about things you wouldn't tell a lot of other people, or give them a hug when they are feeling down. These are all examples of romantic behavior.

Romantic identity terms, like sexual identity terms, often say something about what gender or genders we are drawn to. For example, here are some common romantic identities and their definitions:

Aromantic: Someone who does not experience romantic attraction toward others

Biromantic: Someone who experiences romantic attraction toward people of two (or more) genders

Heteroromantic: Someone who experiences romantic attraction toward people of a gender other than their own

Homoromantic: Someone who experiences romantic attraction toward people of the same gender

Panromantic: Someone who experiences romantic attraction to people of any gender

Again, like sexual identities, romantic identities often don't perfectly match with our romantic attractions or romantic behaviors.

Try It Out!: exploring your sexual and romantic attractions

Have you ever had a crush on someone? Symptoms of a crush can include daydreaming or thinking about a person a lot, having fantasies about being close to that person physically or emotionally, having a funny feeling somewhat like being scared and excited and warm all at once when you talk to them, or avoiding talking to them altogether because they are just that hot! If you have ever had any of these or other symptoms of a crush, describe the qualities of the people you had a crush on that you liked in the space provided. (If you've never had a crush, describe what qualities you think you might be attracted to in a person.)

_____

_____

_____

Do you ever daydream about being close to someone physically or sexually? What happens in these fantasies? Who is in them?

_____

_____

_____

Do you ever daydream about being close to someone emotionally or romantically? What happens in these fantasies? Who is in them?

_____

_____

_____

Do you notice any themes or patterns in what types of people or fantasies you are attracted to?

_____

_____

_____

more about sexual and romantic identities

As you may have noticed above, many of the most common terms about sexual and romantic orientations are defined based on a very simplistic understanding of biological sex and gender.

This can make finding a sexual or romantic identity a little more confusing for people whose gender doesn't fit into these overly simplistic, old-fashioned boxes.

The good news is, like we said above, these labels don't really need to be based on anything except what you decide feels right for you.

For example, take Ting:

Ting is a transgender woman who has always been primarily attracted to men. For many years before she transitioned to living as a woman, Ting lived as a man dating men and was very proud to be part of a strong community of gay men. While Ting's gender identity changed and she began identifying as a woman, she still feels connected to the term "gay" as her sexual identity. Other people sometimes get all confused because she is a woman married to a man and identifies as gay. But Ting knows she doesn't have to explain if she doesn't want to. Those are just the identities that fit for her.

As another example, take Dylan:

Dylan finds ze is romantically attracted to all sorts of people of different gender identities and expressions. Sexually, Dylan finds zirself most attracted to people who don't fit into the gender binary boxes. Since Dylan doesn't like boxes much in general, ze figures either "queer" or "pansexual" might be best to describe zir sexual orientation, if it needs a label at all, and thinks the term "panromantic" applies well to zir.

Finally, take Marty:

Marty changed his sexual orientation identity about a year ago, a little after figuring out more about his gender identity. Once Marty went from living as a girl to living as a boy, he didn't feel like "lesbian" was a good fit for him anymore. Now he identifies as a straight trans man, though he sometimes prefers to say "queer" since he has an understanding of gender that doesn't really fit with the gender binary that "straight" implies.

Finally, many gender diverse people decide that since none of the labels fit them perfectly, they are going to come up with their own definitions of their sexual identity. These identities can be quite creative and fun, or just more accurate than the typical labels. Some examples include:

- A cuddle fanatic

- A human attracted to masculine people

- A lesbian who loves her penis

The point is, the labels are up to you, no matter your attractions or behavior.

Try it Out!: exploring your sexual and romantic identities

On the following page we have provided a table to help you explore your own sexual and romantic identities. Some common identity labels are listed in the far left column. But there are a ton more options out there (including anything you come up with yourself). Feel free to write in other identities that you are considering or have heard of in the blank boxes in the left column. In the middle column discuss why each identity fits and in the far right column discuss why it doesn't.

When exploring the fit of an identity it may help to say it aloud, "I am _____," and then reflect on what thoughts and feelings come up when you say that. Remember, whatever label you come up with can reflect your attractions and behaviors, but it doesn't have to fit perfectly since most people's labels don't anyway.

Identity	Why this does fit for me	Why this does not fit for me
Lesbian		
Gay		
Bisexual		
Heterosexual		
Queer		

Asexual		
Pansexual		
(Other sexual identity label)		
Aromantic		
Biromantic		
Heteroromantic		
Homoromantic		
Panromantic		
(Other romantic identity label)		

Did you find anything that felt like a good fit? Or maybe a few options you think are reasonable? Or maybe this exercise made you realize that you really don't want to label your identity at all?

Whatever feels right for you here is totally fine. And people's identities often evolve over time, so if your thoughts or feelings on this issue change down the road, it is always in your power to change how you define your sexual identity.

dating

Chloe has had a crush on this guy in her chemistry class for several months now. She gets nervous when he is around and never knows what to say to him. He is always friendly with her, but she doesn't know what to make of his friendliness. She wonders, Is he just being nice or does he maybe like me too? *Chloe is not sure if he knows that she is transgender. It has been a while since her transition and no one really talks about it anymore, but she sort of assumes everyone knows. Chloe feels stuck. She wants to tell this guy how she feels, but is afraid he will not be interested in her. On top of that, she doesn't know how in the world to talk to him about being transgender…or even if she should talk to him about being transgender.*

Every time a person starts to date another person, they have to think about how this other person is going to accept the different aspects of who they are. Having a less standard gender identity, wanting to experience gender transition, or having gone through gender transition are all examples of things that can be difficult to figure out how and when to share with a potential partner. For some people, figuring out if, when, and how to share these things becomes so overwhelming that they avoid seeking any intimate relationships, even though they would like to. Or they may give up on relationships before even trying, expecting they will never find someone who will accept them for who they are.

These thoughts and fears are pretty normal for people to have at some point. Happily, most people who want to find a relationship, no matter how unique their current or past gender identity or expression, do find satisfying relationships. And they learn over time how to share their full selves in safe and satisfying ways.

Let's see if we can learn some tips from gender diverse people who have been successful in finding satisfying relationships.

figuring out how, when, or if to come out to potential partners

If your gender identity or experience is different from the standard gender binary, one extra step in dating is figuring out how, when, and if to tell potential partners about your gender identity. For example, let's take Carlos's story:

Carlos is a young trans man. He is going out on a first date with TJ, a guy he met at a gay pride event. When TJ asked him out, he was excited. They didn't have much time to get to know each other at the event, but Carlos found TJ attractive, intelligent, and interesting. Now that he is headed out on this date, though, he has a million questions running through his head: Does he need to tell TJ on their first date that he's trans? Does he wait until they're ready to become sexually intimate? Does he wait until they're starting a committed relationship? What exactly does he need to tell TJ anyway? How is TJ going to respond? Is he still going to be attracted to Carlos?

Carlos's decisions about what to do don't have a right or wrong answer. Different transgender and gender expansive people may approach the same situation in very different ways, depending on what they determine is best for them. Let's think about how to sort through some of these questions to figure out what approach may fit for you.

One question to consider when making the decision about whether or not to come out is: *How soon do I want this person to know about my gender identity or experience and why?* Again, there is no one right answer to this question. You may even approach this question in different ways depending on the person you are interested in dating. You may feel like you want a potential partner to know about your gender identity immediately so that they can make the decision early on about whether they are interested in dating a transgender or gender expansive person. This strategy could help you feel less anxious because you won't feel like you are hiding your true self. It may also help because you won't have to feel stress about anticipating potential rejection at a later time. On the other hand, you may feel like you want this potential partner to get to know you as a person first before knowing about the intimate details of your gender identity. So, when thinking about the person you are interested in dating, what does your gut say about how soon you want to come out to them? Circle the number that most closely matches your current feelings.

1	2	3	4	5
I feel like I need to tell them now! I don't want to move forward with this relationship until the cat is out of the bag!		I think it's best to put this off for a while. I want to feel out the situation as I go.		I don't want to tell them until I'm sure we are interested in each other and we want to be physically intimate.

Based on your answer above, respond to the following questions:

What are the positive parts of making this choice of coming out now or waiting?

_____

_____

_____

What are the negative parts of making this choice?

_____

_____

_____

How might making this choice affect how the relationship moves forward?

_____

_____

_____

_____

After answering these questions, do you still feel the same about your ideas about when to come out? What other thoughts come up in making this decision?

_____

_____

_____

Coming out is challenging because you have to keep making decisions about doing it with each new relationship or with each new person you meet. It's okay (and may in fact be wisest) to make different choices for different relationships and at different times or situations in your life. Make sure only that you come to a decision you feel will be best for you.

safety when talking to partners

Whenever we are having a conversation and are really unsure about what the other person's reaction will be, an important consideration is safety. If you are having a conversation about your gender identity that may catch someone off guard, you need to consider the different potential outcomes. Many people may respond to your gender identity with acceptance. However, it is smart to also consider the possibility of people responding with negativity, or worse, physical aggression or violence. Again, this is not the most typical reaction, but it is necessary to consider the possibility. Below are some tips and questions you can ask yourself as you plan to talk to a potential partner.

Choosing a safe place: When it comes down to the moment when you are talking to this person about a topic such as your gender identity, it is essential that you are in a location that ensures your safety. This safe location may be a public place which would prevent the person from being able to respond loudly or violently. Another option is to come out over the phone, e-mail, or some other form of written or electronic communication. This strategy allows the person to have a response in their own space, separate from you. With this plan, you still want to think about whether or not it is possible that this person could come over to your house or confront you somehow in person after getting off the phone or computer.

What is your plan for choosing a safe place?

_____

_____

_____

_____

Having an exit strategy: After telling this person about your gender identity, you may want to make sure that you are free to leave the situation if you feel uncomfortable or unsafe. For example, you may want to make sure that you are not counting on the other person for a ride home. This is important because they could wait until the car ride to express a negative reaction, or you may understand by their reaction in public that you wouldn't be safe getting in a car with them afterward.

What is your exit strategy?

_____

_____

_____

_____

Checking in with a safety/support person: It may be helpful to have the support of a friend, family member, counselor, or other person while coming out to a potential partner. You may arrange, for example, for this person to know where you are meeting with the potential partner and at what time. You may call or text this person during or after the conversations you have to let them know how it is going. You may also arrange to talk with your support person right after you have finished the conversation. This way, your support person will know whether or not you are in a safe situation and can seek help if needed. Also, you can gain support through this challenging experience.

Who are possible safety/support people?

_____

_____

_____

_____

What is your plan for checking in?

_____

_____

_____

_____

_____

Okay, now you have some ideas about how you want to handle coming out to potential partners and how to keep yourself safe in the process. Now let's think about another dynamic in relationships that can also be both exciting and scary: sex.

sex

Kayla has been in a relationship with her boyfriend, Malik, for over a year now and the relationship is becoming more and more sexual. Malik identifies as bisexual and is very supportive of Kayla's trans identity. But, sometimes Kayla feels like when they are doing sexual activities, Malik touches her body in a way that makes her feel like a boy. This fills her with dysphoria and she immediately pulls away from Malik. This leaves Malik feeling rejected and now sex is becoming a stressful topic in their relationship. Kayla doesn't know how to talk with Malik about her feelings and is afraid she might lose him.

Okay, so sex is a subject many of us have a hard time talking about really openly, especially when it comes to saying specifically what we do and don't like. It makes sense because we are taught that these kinds of conversations are shameful or embarrassing, but it's time to set those messages aside. Communication about sex is super important if you want you and your partner(s) to have satisfying sexual experiences. For example, most people have some things they like their partners to do or say, and other things that just don't make them feel good or don't match with how they think of themselves sexually. And almost everyone has hang-ups about certain parts of their bodies that can get in the way in the bedroom. So no matter what body parts feel right or wrong to you or what ways you do or don't want to be touched, you can still experience a satisfying sexual relationship—it just takes a little exploration and, most importantly, communication.

figuring out what brings you sexual pleasure (and what does not)

Of course, before you can communicate, you need to figure out what could turn you on or give you sexual pleasure and what does not. Some of these things you won't need to try to know that just the idea of them makes you turned on, uncomfortable, or turned off. Other things you might have to try out to see how they feel, given where you are in your life and what type of relationship you are or are not in.

Try It Out!: my turn-ons and turn-offs

What do you already know about yourself sexually? List your turn-ons and turn-offs in the space provided. These can be things that you or your partner do or say or think about, or places or props or videos, or even a type of smell. Everyone is pretty different sexually so you will have to explore for yourself. But we'll give some examples to get you started.

Turn-Ons

Examples: When someone kisses my neck, thinking about having a hard penis, touching someone's chest, when someone smells like coconut, thinking about making out in the water, lying down behind someone, play wrestling, candles, sexy music, feeling romantic and connected to someone

_____

_____

_____

_____

_____

_____

Turn-Offs

Examples: Pink frilly stuff, when someone touches my chest, when a person is aggressive, when a person is very passive, when I dress in more masculine clothes, when a person only seems to care about sex, when someone hasn't brushed their teeth after eating

_____

_____

_____

_____

_____

_____

Sometimes when people feel uncomfortable with their gender identities or the gender expression their body gives them, they can feel hopeless about having a satisfying sexual relationship. While it makes sense to be nervous about this, it turns out there are plenty of creative ways in which you can experience sexual pleasure with a partner. For example, if you don't want someone to touch your genitals, you can utilize other parts of your body that turn you on. If your earlobes are particularly sensitive, you could ask your partner to give you "earlobe blow jobs" instead. Now that's getting creative!

Are there particular body parts that are off limits during sexual activity? If so, what are they?

_____

_____

_____

Are there body parts that can only be touched in certain ways for it to be pleasurable? If so, what are they?

_____

_____

_____

Are there parts of your body outside of genitals that are particularly sensitive for you (for example, neck, ears, back) and might be places to explore sexual pleasure? If so, what are they?

_____

_____

_____

Are there things that you aren't sure how they would feel but might want to try? *Examples:* Wearing a strap-on while my partner cuddles with me on the couch, taking my shirt off but telling my partner I want to keep my bra on, getting or giving an earlobe blow job

_____

_____

_____

Now that you have an idea about your turn-ons and turn-offs, how do you talk with your partner to make sure they know what they are? Let's talk about how to talk about sex.

communication about sex

There are no correct or incorrect answers to the previous questions—however you experience your body sexually is okay. Every person experiences sexuality in their own unique way. However, your partner will not know about your sexual needs and preferences unless you tell them. Even worse, they may continue to try to please you in ways that cause you discomfort. This is why developing good sexual communication is so important. If you are able to voice what sexual activities fit or don't fit for you, and listen to your partners' needs, then you are on track to having satisfying sexual experiences.

Unfortunately, people often feel uncomfortable talking openly and honestly about sex, especially about their own sexual needs and preferences. People often worry that they will feel embarrassed, that their partner will not understand them, that their partner will think they are strange, and so on.

Try It Out!: **let's talk about sex, baby**

What worries or concerns do you have about talking about your sexual needs and preferences?

_____

_____

_____

_____

What potentially good things could come from talking about your sexual needs and preferences?

_____

_____

_____

_____

In order to start these conversations with your partner, it may be helpful to first tell them about your worries and concerns about talking to them. Just expressing concerns can sometimes feel like a relief. You can also ask if they have any things they could tell you. Sometimes you can set up a truth and truth exchange (instead of a truth or dare). You can suggest, "I'll tell you one thing I like if you tell me one thing you like." And then, "I'll tell you one thing I don't like if you trade and tell me one thing you don't like." Your partner may very well be relieved to have a greater understanding of you and how you experience your body. And another perk is that your partner can then also feel freer to talk about what they want and need, which can be helpful to you too!

summary

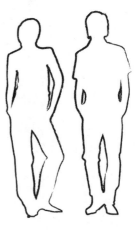

So now that you have explored your own sexual and romantic attractions and identities, as well as strategies for dating and creating satisfying sexual relationships, we hope you feel a little more confident that you can find a relationship that fits with what you want and need. Just know that if you still feel a bit nervous about dating, you are not alone. Dating can be a scary experience for everyone (including all of those people you date who are probably just as nervous about whether you will like them and accept them or not!).

As a final note, many people who don't feel confident in themselves end up "settling" for partners who don't treat them as they would like. They might assume, *Well, this is the best I'm going to get because no one else will be with me.* People sometimes even put up with abusive relationships (emotionally or physically) for this reason. So if you ever find yourself in a relationship that you feel isn't actually what you'd hoped it would be, we hope you will examine your thoughts about yourself and see if you are settling for something that is less than ideal. Chapter 8, Dealing with the Hard Stuff, can be useful for finding help if you are feeling stuck in a relationship and want to change that. It can also help if you're feeling stuck without a relationship. No matter your gender identity or expression, you deserve to find the relationship of your dreams. And despite each of us too having doubted at various points that this was possible for us, we are bringing a message from the future to let you know—your dreams are possible if you don't give up on them!

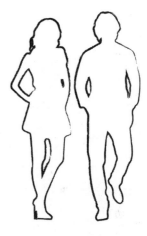

chapter 7

balancing multiple identities

When a person is exploring gender, there are many other parts of identity that can have an effect. For example, your race, ethnicity, religion, ability status, age, and socioeconomic status may all have great impacts on how you navigate your gender journey. These aspects of identity can influence how you experience your gender (your gender identity), how you decide to express your gender (your gender expression), and also how the world reacts to your gender expression.

Let's take a look at two different people to see how these different factors can play out in people's lives.

Eddie is seventeen years old. He is living at home with his family in a small town and hoping to go to college next year. He works part-time at his father's law office, where he is able to make some good money. Eddie is deaf and wants to go to school to become a teacher who works with deaf children. His parents are supportive of this and make a good enough living to support all of Eddie's schooling and medical costs. Eddie and his family attend church regularly and being Christian is an important part of all of their identities. Eddie is white and lives in a community that is primarily white. His mom's side of the family is from England but has been in the United States for many generations. His father is Australian and came to the United States after finishing his law degree.

Jai is fourteen. They live with their mom in a big city. Jai is biracial—half Latino (from their mom's side) and half African American (from their dad's side). Jai works hard in school because they know in order to afford college, they will need to get a scholarship. Jai also has a plan to work once they turn sixteen so they can afford a good school. Jai really wants to be a surgeon someday. Jai and their mom don't really consider themselves religious. They join Jai's father at the Baptist church once in a while so Jai can connect with the strong African American community there.

These two people live very different lives, but both know their gender identities fall somewhere outside of the "male" and "female" boxes that were checked for them when they were born. For each of them, other aspects of identity will intersect with gender and influence their gender identities and expressions.

Some aspects of our identity we spend a lot of time thinking about, and others we do not. Usually, we become most aware of our identity factors that seem different from others. For example, if you identify outside of the gender binary boxes we've been discussing, you are likely to have spent more time thinking about gender than other people your age. Someone like Eddie is likely to have spent more time thinking about his different abilities than someone like Jai, whereas Jai has probably spent more time thinking about race and socioeconomic status than Eddie.

However, just because we haven't spent time thinking about something doesn't mean it isn't an important influence on us.

privilege

One thing our identities impact is our level of privilege. Privilege is a set of advantages given to a certain group of people. For example, Eddie, as a white person in a majority white place, likely has some of the following privileges: learning primarily about the history of his own racial group in school, seeing role models of his own race in the professions he wants to go into, feeling safe when he walks alone in a new place, never wondering whether someone has denied him for a job because of his race, and never being asked to answer questions about white people. Jai, on the other hand, faces some privileges that Eddie does not. For instance, Jai can attend any school without having to request disability services, meet any new person without having to explain or answer questions about deafness, feel confident that their safety is ensured by alarms they can hear (such as fire alarms, car horns, and sirens), and not have to wonder whether someone doesn't want to be their friend just because of a difference in their physical abilities.

Privilege is influenced not just by one identity at a time, but by how our identities relate to each other—what's called intersectionality. For example, we usually think that being a man means you are privileged. While there are certain privileges that all men have, their level of privilege varies based on other factors. For instance, if you're a white man, that usually means you have a high number of privileges. On the other hand, if you're a black man, that means something very different.

Try It Out!: **privilege**

Which of your identities have you spent the most time thinking about?

_____

_____

_____

What identities do you spend the least time thinking about?

_____

_____

_____

In what respects do you think you have privilege?

_____

_____

_____

_____

_____

_____

intersectionality

Even outside of privilege, multiple aspects of our identities relate to our gender identities and expressions in important ways. For example, we learn a lot about what gender options there are and what it means to be a successful representation of that gender from our ethnic and religious communities. These communities may also react in more or less positive ways to our gender identities or expressions.

Let's look back at our examples to see how other identities have intersected with gender to influence Eddie and Jai.

Eddie's father's Australian background and Eddie's church community both have very rigid ideas about what it means to be a boy and a man. Eddie's father had always gotten very angry with Eddie as a boy for not wanting to play sports and for wanting to play dress-up with feminine clothes. Eddie hates wearing a suit for church and would love to grow his hair long, but he is sure it wouldn't go over well there. Eddie therefore has thus far chosen to behave and dress in masculine ways, and even feels a bit ashamed of his wish that he had been born a girl. However, since Eddie has access to his own car and money he's saved, he has been able to meet people a few towns over who support his more feminine identity and expression, and he has bought some more feminine clothes for just these occasions.

Jai's mom is very supportive of Jai's genderqueer identity and expression. Living in a progressive urban area, Jai also receives a good amount of support at school to have gender-neutral bathrooms, use gender-neutral pronouns, and be themselves. However, Jai worries that they will face discrimination in finding a job or in getting into college in the future. Jai is also becoming more uncomfortable with how their body is changing now that puberty has started. Because Jai's family isn't wealthy, they don't have access right now to psychologists or medical doctors to help Jai deal with this anxiety or think about any medical interventions that may make Jai feel more comfortable with their body.

As you can see, both of these people's experiences of their gender and decisions about gender expression have been significantly influenced by other aspects of their identities.

So what about you? Let's look at how different aspects of your identity relate to your gender experience and expression.

race and ethnicity

Race is sort of like gender in that it is something that we think of as having factual biological categories, but in reality it isn't so clear-cut. When we talk about race, we are usually referring to inherited physical characteristics that make a person appear as "white," "black," "Asian," and so on. A person can be multiracial, having two or more races represented in their inherited physical characteristics.

Ethnicity, on the other hand, relates to your culture instead of your biologically inherited traits. Culture can be defined in many ways and so people may define their ethnicity based on nation, continent, or other group-defining factors. For example, a person who is white could be of many different ethnicities, such as Eastern European, South African, or Jewish. A person who is black might identify as African American, Haitian, or Latino. A person who is Asian might identify as Chinese, Japanese, or Filipino. Then of course, people may have multiple ethnicities that are all important parts of their identities. There are endless possibilities.

Race and ethnicity are central factors in the way we experience the world, the way we are treated, and the values and beliefs we learn.

Try It Out!: racial and ethnic identity

Let's spend some time thinking about your racial and ethnic identities and how they relate to your gender:

What racial and ethnic communities are you a part of?

_____

_____

_____

_____

What is considered to be "normal" with respect to gender in your racial and ethnic communities?

_____

_____

_____

_____

What have you learned in your racial and ethnic communities about people who have gender identities or gender expressions that are different from what is considered "normal"?

_____

_____

_____

_____

_____

Can you envision your gender identity or expression changing in any ways in the future? If so, list the ways. Next to each, write how you expect people in your racial and ethnic communities may react to these changes:

_____

_____

_____

_____

_____

How are your racial and ethnic communities' values similar to your own values regarding gender? How are they different? How do you balance these differences?

_____

_____

_____

_____

_____

How does your gender identity and expression influence how much you feel you belong with people in your racial and ethnic communities?

_____

_____

_____

_____

_____

Ideally, everyone could be their full self with regard to gender and race and ethnicity in all contexts and be accepted for who they are everywhere. However, many of our different racial and ethnic communities will have an understanding of gender and sexuality that may not match our own. A person may therefore face some choices to balance their gender identity (such as transgender or genderqueer) and their racial or ethnic identity (such as black, Latino, Asian, and so on). For example, Jai might feel pretty sure that being their full genderqueer self will mean rejection from the community of African American peers they hang out with at their father's church community, and so they might adjust how they dress there. Being subjected to his father's Australian cultural beliefs about how all men should be very macho, Eddie might feel that he should continue dressing in more masculine ways around his father. Both Jai and Eddie may choose to dress differently or not discuss their gender identity with people in specific communities. They may find other spaces and communities where they can dress to fully express their gender and feel safe and supported. There is nothing wrong with making these choices to represent your gender more or less openly in different settings. We all show different parts of ourselves to different people.

However, it can be hard to find the right balance of identities and communities alone. We recommend trying to find other people who have faced or are facing similar decisions to your own, so you can learn from how they have navigated these choices or navigate them together. There are many ways to find people, but a great place to start is online. You can search for groups, e-mail listservs, books, blogs, videos, and other resources. Hearing other people's experiences can help you realize you are not alone while giving you some ideas about what might work well to balance your identities in your life.

Depending on what identities you connect with, you might want to spend more or less time on the following sections. Sometimes it's eye-opening to work through a section even if it isn't something that feels really important to you. You might either discover something about an aspect of yourself that you rarely think about, or better understand other people in your life. But as always, it's totally up to you to read and complete whatever parts of the book you want.

religion

For some of us, our religious identity is an important aspect of who we are. Others don't feel connected to a particular religion, but still likely have certain things they value or believe to be of importance in their lives. Our religious beliefs and values might be in line with our gender identities and expressions, or they may also seem in conflict. For example, some religions support a binary understanding of gender and value masculine men and feminine women. They may teach that people who don't fit into this binary are sinful, wrong, or even sick. Someone who doesn't fit into these boxes might feel like they need to choose between their religion and their gender. Luckily, most people, regardless of their religion, find a way to fit their beliefs and gender together, even if it isn't easy at first. Other people have beliefs and values that are not in conflict with their gender, but still serve as important influences on how they understand their gender and what choices they make regarding gender expression. So let's explore below.

Try It Out!: religion

Were you taught any lessons about gender from a particular religion or belief system?

_____

_____

_____

_____

_____

Compare what you learned above with your own current beliefs about gender. How are your current beliefs similar? How are your current beliefs different?

_____

_____

_____

_____

_____

Values are the things that are most important to us. Many people feel their values are connected to their religion, while other people feel their values are more independently driven. Look at the list of values below. Circle five to ten values that are most important to you.

- Abundance: Having more than enough of what you need

- Accomplishment: Reaching remarkable achievements

- Affection: Showing love and warmth

- Beauty: Focusing on things that are aesthetically pleasing

- Calm: Quiet and peace

- Caution: Being careful

- Challenge: Being pushed to do more or be better

- Community: Being part of and participating in a group of people with whom you share something in common

- Compassion: Showing kindness

- Contentment: Being calm and at peace with what you have

- Courage: Being brave

- Creativity: Imagination

- Curiosity: Eagerness to know more

- Discipline: Being able to maintain good control over yourself to achieve goals

- Excitement: Lively enjoyment

- Expression: Conveying thoughts and feelings

- Faith: Trust in beliefs

- Fame: Being very well known

- Family: Focusing on those you're related to

- Freedom: Being able to make choices to be and act as you wish

- Friends: Being with people that you care about

- Fun: Enjoying yourself

- Generosity: Being willing to give to others

- Genuineness: Being real and sincere

- Growth: Focusing on becoming better

- Happiness: Lively contentment

- Health: Being in good physical and mental condition

- Honesty: Telling the truth

- Industry: Getting things done, building, or creating

- Justice and fairness: Equality and lack of bias

- Knowledge and learning: Continuing to gain information and intellectual growth in school or out

- Love: Giving and receiving care and affection

- Loyalty: Faithfulness to others

- Mastery: High levels of skill

- Peace: Absence of conflict

- Practicality: Focusing on facts

- Recognition: Being acknowledged and appreciated

- Relaxation: Time for resting

- Respect: Holding yourself and others with esteem, or being held in esteem by others

- Romance: The expression of feelings of excitement related to love

- Safety: Being protected from harm, emotionally or physically

- Thrift: Being careful with money and finances

- Insert your own unlisted value here: _____

- Insert your own unlisted value here: _____

For the values circled, how do they relate to your religious beliefs, identity, and practices?

_____

_____

_____

_____

For the values you circled above, how do they relate to your gender identity and expression?

_____

_____

_____

_____

Are there ways your values can help you tie together your religious and gender identities and expressions? Are there ways your religion or gender still feel in conflict with your values?

_____

_____

_____

_____

For some, learning how to balance religion and gender can take a while. It can be helpful to talk to other people about how they fit together their religion and their gender. There are many ways in which to do this, including holding onto your beliefs but changing where you go to worship, staying in your current religious community but holding some different beliefs from others around you, being a voice that helps other people in your religious community understand different gender identities and experiences, or holding onto your values but making changes in your religious practices or gender expression to reflect these values. Whatever your path turns out to be is okay, and like we said, it may take you some time to find what fits for you. Take your time and don't stop searching for that balance that leads you to a place of feeling at peace with your beliefs and your identities.

socioeconomic status

Socioeconomic status is yet another piece of identity that influences the exploration and understanding of gender. Again, people who are not in a position of economic privilege (people who have don't have a lot of money) will probably have spent more time thinking about economic status and how it relates to their gender identity or expression. Youth especially can face financial challenges for a number of reasons, such as not having jobs with enough income, or not having family support. In terms of gender, this can influence things like having access to a therapist to help explore your gender identity, having access to a medical doctor to help you make any physical changes to your gender expression, having the ability to live independently of an unsupportive family, having money for a legal name change, and having money for a new wardrobe that suits your gender.

Others have some privilege in this area and their choices may seem less influenced by money. However, even people with high economic privilege may face economic, gender-related pressures. For example, someone from a family that is quite wealthy may face expectations that they will prioritize a career that affords them a similar lifestyle. Any perceived risk to such a career, including holding a nonbinary gender identity, may be particularly frowned upon.

So again, you see we are all affected by intersecting identities. Let's see how your socioeconomic status affects your gender identity and expression.

Try It Out!: socioeconomic status

Are there gender-related pressures you face because of your socioeconomic status?

_____

_____

_____

Are there any parts of your gender exploration that will cost money?

_____

_____

_____

Sometimes, as desperately as we want something, we may not be able to afford it or access it right away because of money. This can be really hard when you want something so badly! **When this is the case, it helps to make a plan for how you can get what you want in the future.**

If you are in a position of not being able to afford everything you'd like to try, which things are the most important or the most urgent to you?

_____

_____

_____

Use the space below to brainstorm ideas about how you might eventually save up for your desired items.

Ideas for making and saving money:

_____

_____

_____

_____

Depending on how quickly you think you can earn money and how much what you desire costs, you might have to work toward your goal for a shorter or longer time. In the meantime, when you are feeling desperate to keep moving on your gender journey, it helps to remember there are plenty of things you can do, no matter your socioeconomic status, that don't take a lot of money.

Take some time to brainstorm ways you can take steps towards being yourself that are in your budget (or even free).

Examples: Borrow a friend's clothes and go out together, look into different insurance options to see what coverage you might get at different future jobs, buy men's or women's deodorant next time you need more, change your hairstyle, talk to someone new about your gender, use a different name when you order something at a restaurant, dance like a boy/girl, and everything in between.

What things can you think of?

_____

_____

_____

_____

_____

_____

other identity factors

By now we've covered a few identity factors in depth, but we certainly haven't covered all of the things that are important to different people. Are there other identities you hold that have some influence on your gender identity or expression (such as your age or your ability status)?

_____

_____

_____

_____

For each factor you listed, tell us about how it relates to your gender identity and gender expression:

_____

_____

_____

_____

_____

_____

_____

_____

_____

_____

_____

summary

Clearly our identities are pretty complicated. What we've found is that since our identities change and evolve over time, we are constantly exploring what it means to be ourselves in the different places, times, and contexts we are in. So just because you completed this chapter (round of applause!), don't feel like the fun stops here! Get ready for a lifetime of identity exploration. The really cool thing is, by understanding that each identity you have doesn't work alone—that instead they all intersect—you're much wiser about identity than a lot of people and ready to explore your identities in really perceptive ways. Enjoy!

chapter 8

dealing with the hard stuff

Most of us have our fair share of stress on a daily basis just dealing with school or work, friends and family relationships, and other regular life stuff. Sometimes life seems like a juggling act—with each of these responsibilities, another ball to keep up in the air. When you have the number of balls you're able to juggle, this can be a fun challenge. But then, throw another ball into the mix and life can become overwhelming.

Let's just say gender can bring a lot of balls into the mix for you to juggle!

In this chapter we'll talk truth about some of the hard stuff that people face related to gender identity and gender expression. We'll also talk about how people deal with this hard stuff so you can navigate future stress like a champ.

the stress of stepping outside of your "comfort zone"

So where has your Gender Quest taken you? Have you found yourself in unexpected places? Having different experiences, thoughts, feelings? This new stuff can be exciting. But let's be honest, this process can also be extremely stressful!

Going on a Gender Quest means stepping outside of your "comfort zone." Your comfort zone contains the things (experiences, people, places, thoughts, and feelings) that you are used to experiencing and managing. It's pretty comfy-cozy in that comfort zone—kind of like staying in bed in your PJs. If you are reading this book, you've already gotten the courage to get out from under the covers and see what's going on outside. Congratulations—this means your life will be way more interesting and you will be way wiser than if you'd stayed in bed in your PJs your whole life!

But getting out of your comfort zone can obviously also mean experiencing uncomfortable things. You may discover new thoughts and feelings about your gender.

Many of these thoughts might feel good. It's also normal to experience stressful thoughts. Some common stressful thoughts people experience when exploring their gender include:

This is so confusing!

Why can't other people understand?

Can I really wear that?

I hate my body.

What if I can never be my true self?

I wish there was a test to tell me my gender.

Does this mean there is something wrong with me?

I wish there were no such thing as gender.

What will happen if I tell people how I feel?

Why am I like this?

Does this mean I have to stop playing baseball?

Does this mean I need to stop liking pink?

I wish I were normal…whatever that means.

While it is natural for people to feel excited, relieved, optimistic, and eager when they start exploring gender, difficult feelings can also arise. Some common difficult feelings people experience when exploring their gender include:

- Fear/Nervousness

- Overwhelm

- Shame

- Anger

- Hopelessness

- Insecurity

- Jealousy/Resentment

- Loneliness

- Grouchiness/Irritability

- Sadness

- Inferiority

- Depression

Try It Out!: thoughts and feelings

One way to deal with difficult or stressful thoughts and feelings is to notice that there's a difference between thoughts and feelings.

Thoughts are:

Sentences or words that you can almost hear being said in your head. We all have this inner voice—it's our brains thinking. These thoughts can be helpful to us, or unhelpful.

Here are some examples of thoughts that many people have:

I'll never figure this out.

No one will love me.

I can't wait to finish transition.

This is awesome!

I'm finally getting to be myself.

Feelings, on the other hand, are emotions and moods we experience. People experience feelings in many ways. You may have noticed that you feel sadness as a weight in your chest, or that you feel hot when you're angry. You might smile or feel a bright feeling in your stomach when you're excited. People often cry or tear up when sad. Hearts can pound when people are excited and when they're scared. People may clench their fists or tense other muscles when angry. Our bodies and feelings are closely connected.

Here are some examples of feelings that most everyone experiences:

- Angry
- Happy
- Sad
- Confident
- Anxious

- Victorious

- Frustrated

- Joyful

- Impatient

- Proud

- Irritable

- Excited

So thoughts and feelings are different, but they are also often connected. Often our thoughts lead to feelings.

For example, the thought *Everyone at school would laugh at me if they saw me wearing that* might go along with feelings of fear or shame or even anger.

The thought *Hey, I look pretty darn good in this new outfit*! might go along with feelings of excitement, pride, and happiness.

Think back on the thoughts and feelings you've had during your Gender Quest. Since we're in the Dealing with the Hard Stuff chapter, let's focus on the stressful ones. Write down any stressful thoughts and feelings that have come up below. Then draw lines connecting the thoughts with the different feelings that went together for you at that time.

Thoughts	Feelings

the tricky brain

One thing you may notice is that thoughts and feelings change over time. Are there thoughts and feelings from the previous section that don't feel as intense now as they did at the time? Circle any thoughts and feelings that are less stressful for you in this moment than they were at some point in the past.

When thoughts remain stubbornly stressful over time, they can begin to weigh us down. Luckily, now we know thoughts and feelings do change over time. The question is, can we change our thoughts and feelings, or understand them in a different way, so we feel less weighed down?

Yes, we can. Now this is some advanced stuff we're about to get into—changing and understanding brains without any surgeries or drugs or medical degrees. Kind of like the most powerful tool ever! But we figure you should be in on the secret about handling our tricky brains, and we hope you will use these brain-changing powers for good.

So here's the deal with thoughts and feelings.

- *What we experience in our brains is often not completely accurate.* Our brains are great at dealing with large amounts of information—categorizing and rating things as good or bad, safe or dangerous, yummy or disgusting. But really, these judgments and categories that our brain has aren't *real*. For example, brussels sprouts exist. They are a fact, like it or not. Now when you put a brussels sprout in your mouth and let your brain experience it, your brain could have all sorts of thoughts and feelings about that innocent sprout. One of the authors of this book absolutely loves brussels sprouts. When he eats them, his brain thinks *Good, yummy, delicious,* and he feels happy and content. When this same author was ten, when his same brain was confronted with brussels sprouts, it would start firing *Yuck! Disgusting! Terrible!* He would feel sick and woeful and angry that the world ever created such sprouts.

- *Even though thoughts and feelings aren't facts, our brains tell us that they are and we usually believe our brains.* For example, the author at ten was convinced that brussels sprouts were inarguably disgusting. He believed that this was a truth you could not argue with, and he thought anyone who didn't think the same thing was just plain wrong.

- *Certain types of thoughts and feelings are more likely to not only be inaccurate, but also to get us into trouble.* While we can't go around questioning and evaluating every thought we have for accuracy, it is useful to know some common tricks brains play that can lead to trouble. Here's a list:

  - *Using all-or-nothing language.* Whenever you hear your thoughts contain words like *everyone, no one, always,* or *never*. For example, if your brain says *Everyone laughs at me,* or *Things never go my way,* beware. These thoughts are usually inaccurate and often unhelpful.

  - *Fortune-telling.* Whenever you hear your brain predicting the future. For example, when you hear yourself thinking *I'll never get to have the body I want,* or *College is going to be too hard,* again, beware. These thoughts are also often inaccurate and unhelpful.

  - *Mind reading.* Whenever you hear your brain telling you what someone else thinks. For example, *They think I look ridiculous,* or *She hates me.* You know the drill by now—beware. Inaccurate. Unhelpful.

  - *Labelling.* Whenever you hear your brain labelling a situation or person (including labelling yourself). For example, *I'm an idiot,* or *That's so stupid.* Beware. Potentially inaccurate and unhelpful.

  - *Shoulds and Have-Tos.* Whenever you hear your brain telling you that you "should" or "have to" do something, it is also useful to examine it for accuracy and helpfulness. For example, *I should wear a bike helmet* is a helpful thought; it increases your odds of carrying an intact brain into the future. However, less helpful shoulds and have-tos appear in statements like *I shouldn't have told her yet,* or *I have to get hormones soon.*

- *By writing down or talking about your thoughts and evaluating them for whether they are accurate and helpful, you can loosen the power that stressful thoughts have in weighing you down.* You may find that by going through the process of questioning your thoughts, you actually change what you believe and how it makes you feel. Or you may find that the thought is still there, but since you know the thought isn't fully accurate, or at least not helpful, you are able to let it affect you less.

So let's play around with your new brain powers.

Try It Out!: brain change

Look back at your list of stressful thoughts from the last exercise. First, do any of the common brain tricks show up in your thoughts? If yes, list some here:

_____

_____

_____

_____

Consider how you could make these thoughts a bit more accurate and helpful. Many times our unhelpful thoughts can be changed to something that's constructive or at least helps us cope. For example, *Everyone at school would laugh at me if they saw me wearing that* might change to: *Some people might laugh, but I know my friends won't. And they will stick up for me.*

Try it here:

Unhelpful Thought	Challenge to Thought
My mom will totally freak out if I tell her I'm trans.	My mom's first reaction will probably be to think and say that I'm going through a phase and she might want me to see a psychologist. But she wouldn't kick me out or stop talking to me or anything like that. And if she were angry at first, that doesn't mean she wouldn't adjust over time.
Unhelpful Thought	Challenge to Thought

Notice: Do your feelings change as you challenge your thoughts? Is it hard or easy to change them?

You may wish to turn back to this section as you listen more to your thoughts to check them for brain tricks. Like any new skill, brain-changing skills require practice. We highly recommend that you practice by writing down your thoughts and seeing what your brain is thinking on paper. If you do this once a day, or even once a week, you can become an all-powerful brain-changing master.

gender minority stress

Like we said earlier, we all usually have enough stress just from our regular life. But for people belonging to groups that experience stigma or prejudice (because of race, class, ability level, gender, or other factors), we face additional stress called "minority stress." Minority stress happens when people of a minority group experience things like bullying, discrimination, violence, harassment, or rejection because they are a member of a minority group. These minority stressors don't happen to everyone in a minority group. But even if you don't experience something yourself, you may be stressed just by the thought that it could happen to you.

"Gender minority stress" also occurs when people treat us in ways that don't match with our gender identities. For example, if people call you "he" when you know yourself to be a she, call you by your birth name after you have changed to a name of a different gender, or treat you like a gender you don't identify with, it can be super stressful (or just plain annoying)! All of these "little things" can add up to a serious amount of distress that impacts us just like other minority stressors.

Try It Out!: **minority stress**

Have you ever heard of someone facing discrimination, victimization, or rejection because of their race, class, ability level, or gender? Perhaps someone was a victim of violence or bullying, perhaps others didn't want to be their friend, or maybe you saw someone being made fun of on a TV show or in a movie. Write down any instances that come to mind.

_____

_____

_____

_____

Pick one instance that sticks out to you. What did you think and feel at the time?

_____

_____

_____

_____

Maybe you can see above how even when something doesn't happen directly to us, minority stress can make an impact on us.

consequences of gender minority stress

As you can imagine, if you have had any of these minority stress things happen to you directly, the impact can be even stronger. When people think about the times they've experienced minority stress, they often have stressful thoughts and feelings come up.

There are three types of reactions to minority stress that are quite common and have been given names.

- Internalized Transphobia

  Whether or not we want to, we all learn from the stereotyped and prejudiced images and messages we see around us. Women hold the stereotypes and prejudices they've been taught about women. Men hold the stereotypes and prejudices they've been taught about men. And—you guessed it—transgender and gender expansive people hold stereotypes about transgender and gender expansive people. This is bad news not only for how we view others, but for how we view ourselves. When we "internalize" (or believe) "transphobic" things, like *Transgender people are crazy*, *Masculine women are ugly*, or *Feminine men are inferior*, we also end up feeling that *we* are crazy or ugly or inferior. As you can imagine, this isn't too good for your self-esteem.

- Negative Expectations About Future Events

  Not surprisingly, if someone has been harassed, bullied, rejected, or been a victim of violence in the past, they may worry that it could happen again; some people even start to expect that it will happen again. This expectation can be there even if you've just heard of something happening to someone like yourself, but haven't been a victim yourself. Having negative expectations can show up in multiple ways. Some examples are:

  - Not introducing yourself to new people because you fear they will make fun of you

  - Not applying for a job because you expect they will discriminate against you

  - Not coming out to family or friends because you believe they will reject you.

  When the world seems hostile, it can be hard to figure out when there is a really good chance of danger or rejection and when it is a good idea to take a chance and put yourself out there.

- Staying "closeted"

  For people who decide the world is not a safe place to be themselves, they may choose to not disclose or show their full wonderful selves to the world. For example, people may decide that they need to continue wearing clothes that don't feel like they fit, or keep a name and pronouns that don't feel right, or not let certain people find out how they really feel about themselves and their gender. There is nothing wrong with deciding to do these things. Sometimes it is even wise or necessary to keep yourself safe. And, it turns out that having to hold back in this way can add up over time to be a major stressor.

signs of stress

When you add up all of the minority stressors we just talked about, and the impact on how we think about ourselves, you can get some serious consequences. As a result, people of stigmatized groups (including racial, ethnic, economic, and gender minorities) are at higher risk for mental health and physical health problems.

In terms of mental health, people who have experienced minority stress are more likely to experience the stress as depression or anxiety. Some people even start to feel suicidal as a result. Long-term stress can impact your physical health as well.

Try It Out!: **stress test**

Do you see any signs of stress in yourself?

Check yes or no for the things you have experienced over the past month:

Yes	No	
☐	☐	Feeling down or depressed
☐	☐	Crying easily
☐	☐	Feeling overwhelmed
☐	☐	Having frequent stomachaches or headaches
☐	☐	Having no appetite or eating more than you would like
☐	☐	Having trouble sleeping or sleeping too much
☐	☐	Feeling anxious or on edge
☐	☐	Feeling like your heart is pounding or you are having trouble breathing
☐	☐	Using alcohol or other drugs more than you or others think you should
☐	☐	Wishing you weren't alive

If you said no to all of the above, fantastic!

What happens if you answered yes to some of the above, though? Or even a lot of them? Well, first of all, bravo and brava for being courageous enough to tell it like it is. It's not easy to see how stress is taking its toll. The first thing to know is you are not alone; in fact, we wouldn't have dedicated a whole chapter to this stuff if there weren't a whole lot of people also in your shoes. We get it. While our stories are each unique, we have each faced stress that overwhelms us at times. It wasn't always easy to deal with it all, so we share below some things that helped us on our paths, with the hope they may help you too.

dealing with stress

The good news is that there are ways to work with this stress to reduce it and the impact it has on you. We all have our own ways of dealing with stress. That's because different things work well for each of us. There are so many things to try, we've each only discovered some of the many things that probably work for us. For example, one of our friends even swears that brushing her teeth helps her calm down if she is feeling anxious or worried!

A lot of people call the ways you deal with stress your "coping skills." People can have both positive and negative coping skills.

Positive coping skills help us feel better without damaging our bodies, lives, or relationships with others. Listening (or singing) to music, painting or drawing, watching a favorite movie, baking, talking to a friend, and spending time with a pet are all examples of positive coping skills.

Negative coping skills may make a person feel better temporarily. But the problem with negative coping skills is in the long term, they often make you feel worse, or damage your health or your relationships. Examples of negative coping skills are taking drugs, bingeing on ice cream, being mean to your little brother, or punching the wall.

What are some positive coping skills you like to use?

_____

_____

_____

_____

The other good thing to keep in mind about coping skills is that different things work for different emotions and situations. For example, for a lot of people, when they're feeling hurt or confused by something, talking to someone they trust can be most helpful. But some of those same people, when they're really sad, won't want to talk to anyone and may find they want to be alone. What helps them in those moments might be listening to music or writing about what is going on in their journal. If they're angry, on the other hand, they might find that exercise works better than anything else.

So, this means that in order to become a coping master, you have to (1) figure out what emotion you are feeling, and (2) use one of your best coping strategies for that emotion.

figuring out emotions

Step 1: Figuring out emotions. Believe it or not, this part can be tricky. Often we are feeling more than one thing at the same time, but we may only think about the one that seems the most intense. That's why it can be helpful to practice. You can practice as much as you want (we suggest a daily check-in journal) to find out what you are feeling.

Try It Out!: emotions journal

Find a journal for yourself. It can be an actual notebook; or a phone, which a lot of people use so they can journal wherever they are. The key is, it should be something that you are confident only you will have access to. There are many ways of journaling, but one of the most simple and effective things is to just write about whatever thoughts pop into your head. Like we said above, many thoughts aren't anything very profound. But that doesn't matter. When you are journaling your "stream of consciousness" like this, all that matters is that you keep writing whatever thought pops into your head. Journaling is something that helps us recognize what our thoughts and feelings are. This seems like it should be plain to see. But the more you start journaling, the more you will see that our heads are very complicated places. Thoughts and emotions zoom by sometimes quicker than we can notice if we aren't paying close attention. By writing, we can slow down just enough to discover some very interesting things about ourselves.

Start with five minutes of journaling right now. If you haven't decided on a journal yet, that's okay, just get some paper and a pen. Ready, set, flow…

Has it been five minutes yet? No?! Well, get back to journaling then! You can even write "I don't know what else to write." Just keep putting down whatever is in your head.

Now look at the illustrations on the opposite page. How many emotions did you experience in those five minutes? Were there emotions under those emotions? Circle all that you felt.

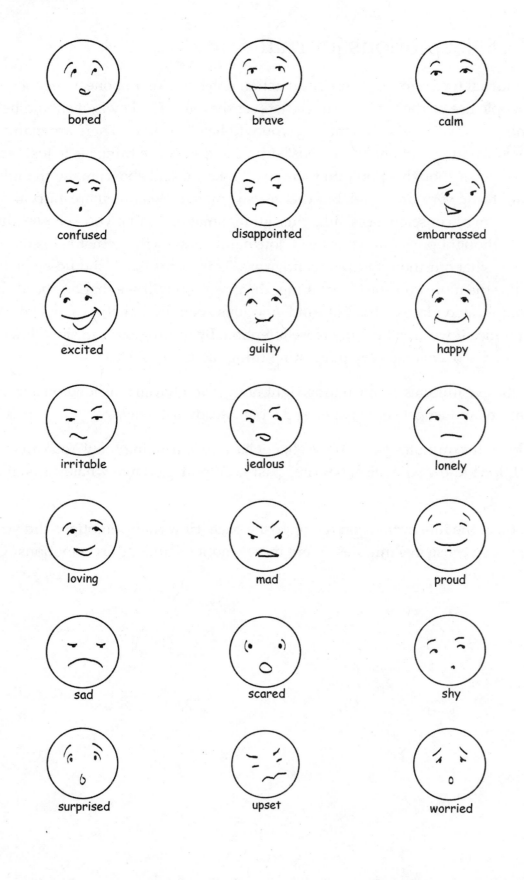

Try It Out!: coping with different emotions

Step 2: Here's the part where you get to be creative.

Pick five difficult or negative emotions you think you feel most often and list them on the left side below. Then on the right side, list your coping skills—both positive and negative. If you are stuck, look at the list of coping skills in the appendix.

Emotion	Positive Coping Skills I Know Work	Any Negative Coping Skills I Have Used	New Positive Coping Skills I Could Try
Example: Sad	Listening to music, writing in my journal, crying, looking at funny YouTube videos	Overeating, isolating myself (both feel good temporarily but seem to make me feel worse over time)	Talking to someone, painting

It's handy to have this list when you are feeling intense emotions. For many of us, when we are feeling intense emotions, we lose sight of all of the positive coping skills we could try. And sometimes negative coping skills that we are used to using can seem hard to resist.

Get a blank index card or other piece of paper that will be pretty sturdy and can fit in your wallet. (You can cut construction paper to the right size if you don't have an index card.) Draw and list your different positive coping skills so you can have a reminder with you wherever you are. Now decorate your card however you wish with doodles, stickers, and collage pictures that inspire you to connect with the part of yourself that is strong, hopeful, and resilient!

when do I need more help?

All of us get in over our heads sometimes. Life is long. Sometimes there will be really awesome stretches where things are just great—the sun seems to shine brighter, things go our way, and we just feel good. Then sometimes there can be really rough stretches that seem like they'll never end, when the sky looks grey and nothing seems to go our way. So many things may come at us at once that we just can't keep up with them by using our coping skills.

Here are some signs that you are overwhelmed and need more help:

- You feel hopeless.

- Your feel irritable or tearful a lot of the time.

- You wish you weren't alive anymore.

- You want to run away or escape your life.

- You have started cutting or harming yourself.

- You can't sleep or want to sleep all the time.

- You've stopped going to school or work sometimes.

- You've stopped doing things that you used to enjoy.

- You are using potentially dangerous coping skills, like:

  - Drugs more than you think is good for you

  - Alcohol more than you think is good for you

  - Sex in a way that you don't think is good for you

  - Eating (or not eating) in a way that you don't think is good for you.

If any of the above are happening and your positive coping skills aren't working, it's probably time to reach out.

where can I get help?

If you are reading this book, you're likely to want to find some help that will be friendly to your concerns about gender as well as your other needs.

There are many options for getting help. Some of the most common are finding an online group of people who are going through similar things, finding an in-person support group of people going through similar things, calling a hotline, and seeing a therapist or counselor.

group support

It turns out, one of our core needs as humans is to feel understood. Often, it is easier for people who have gone through something at least somewhat similar to us to understand what we are thinking and feeling. You can find people like this in support forums and support groups. The easiest way to find both is to search online for what is in your area. Not all groups are good ones, though. You have to find one that feels like the right fit for you. Before you enter, you can usually contact the group leader and talk to them to see whether it will be a good group for you.

Going to a new group makes *everyone* nervous. But once you try a few and find one that feels right, it is worth that initial courage. So remember, use whatever coping skills work for you when you are feeling nervous, and get yourself there—whether it's online or in person.

hotlines

We highly recommend hotlines such as The Trevor Project: 1-866-488-7386, Trans Lifeline: 1-877-565-8860 (US) / 1-877-330-6366 (Canada), or the National Suicide Prevention Lifeline: 1-800-273-8255. Hotlines aren't there just for when you are in an acute crisis or feeling suicidal. For example, about 80% of people who call Trans Lifeline are just looking for support or information about being transgender. So if you're just feeling overwhelmed or want some more support, give a hotline a try. Calling The Trevor Project should get you someone who knows specifically about LGBTQ youth stuff, and calling Trans Lifeline should get you someone who won't flinch at any trans-related stuff. You can find some other helpful information in the list of resources available at the website for this book.

therapists

Finding a therapist who can work with gender diverse people can be easy or hard depending on where you live. Often, a good place to start is by word of mouth. Do you have friends or family who know of a therapist who they think will be a good fit for you?

You might also call a local LGBT center or visit their website. They often have referrals to local therapists.

Other people start with the internet. GoodTherapy.org (http://www.goodtherapy .org/) and Psychology Today (https://www.psychologytoday.com) are national websites that list therapists who are knowledgeable about LGBTQ issues.

Finally, if you are going through an insurance company, you can call them and ask for referrals to local therapists that work with LGBTQ people.

Once you get some names, you should call the therapist and talk with them on the phone. You can ask them if they have experience working with transgender and/or genderqueer people and if they have experience working on the issues you might want to discuss in therapy. If they sound like they might be a good fit, then you can talk about fees. And if that seems to work for you, you can go ahead and make an appointment. If they don't seem like a good fit or you can't afford them, you can ask them if they have any other names for people in your area that you could try.

In your first few appointments, the person will probably ask you a lot of questions to try to understand what is going on for you and how they might help. It is also a good time for you to ask all of the questions you have about therapy. Just because you see someone once doesn't mean you need to go back. You can use the first few sessions as time to test how it feels to talk to them. If it seems like it might be helpful, keep it up! If not, you can leave at any time. Keep in mind that talking to a stranger can seem odd or even scary at first. We encourage people going to therapy for the first time to try to stick with it and give it a chance, even if it feels slightly uncomfortable.

In that first phone call, you can also ask about your rights to confidentiality. If you are under eighteen, you might be concerned about whether the therapist might tell your parents or guardians something you don't want them to know. The point of therapy is to have a safe space to confidentially talk, so therapists as a rule take confidentiality very seriously. They can even lose their license if they break it. However, there are exceptions where therapists need to break confidentiality to make sure everyone is safe. These exceptions to confidentiality are a little different depending on what state you live in and how old you are. So don't hesitate to ask your therapist about this (and any other concerns you have) before starting therapy.

when to seek emergency care

Obviously, you know that if you just broke a bone, you should probably go to the Emergency Room (ER). But a lot of people don't know that if they are feeling really desperate or unsafe, they can also go to the ER. What does really desperate or unsafe mean? If you think there is a real chance you may seriously hurt yourself, harm someone else, or do something that could result in your death, this is a time to either (1) call a hotline to have them help you figure out what to do and where to go or (2) go directly to the closest ER and explaining what is going on.

Some people are afraid of how they will be treated at the ER because of their gender identity or expression. If this is true for you, please consider bringing someone you trust with you. Alternatively, you can call either The Trevor Project or the Trans Lifeline and problem-solve with them how you might get help without exposing yourself to more minority stress.

summary

We hope this chapter has given you some extra knowledge and skills to equip you on your lifelong Gender Quest. We bet that if you journal, you will end up describing some amazingly wonderful experiences as well as some hard times. This is all part of any quest. We hope you will remember that not just us but many other people are by your side on your journey. You can check out what's out there in the list of resources at the website for this book: http://www.newharbinger.com/32974. Our best wishes for your continuing explorations!

conclusion

We hope this workbook has given you some extra knowledge and skills to equip you on your lifelong Gender Quest. We bet that you will end up having some amazingly wonderful experiences on your quest as well as some hard times. Any good quest has all of the above. Think of Luke Skywalker in *Star Wars*, or Harry Potter, or Katniss Everdeen in *The Hunger Games*, or whomever your favorite hero or heroine is. On each of their quests there were days they were doubtful or desperate and days they were confident and triumphant. They never knew where the road would eventually lead them, and yet they kept going forward a day at a time. We join you on this lifelong journey—following our own individual quests through the ups and downs of life, wondering where we will find ourselves in the end, and occasionally looking back in amazement at where we've been. We hope you will remember we are by your side, and we are glad to know you are walking alongside us too!

afterword
by Arlene Lev

All of life is truly a quest—a journey and explorative odyssey—to define, invent, discover, and create a unique self, one that reflects our inner experience. In the modern world we know this is true about jobs and careers, about dress style, interests, and even finding love—young people are encouraged to think about what they want to do when they grow up, supported to dress in ways they feel comfortable, urged to explore after-school interests like theater and athletics, and are even cautioned to choose their love interests carefully from all the available people they can possibly date. Exploration is indeed our expectation for youth.

However, for most professionals, gender has been seen as more of a fact of biology than part of a quest of identity. As young people increasingly identify as genderqueer and pansexual, and actively choose which pronouns they prefer— he, she, or they—adults often find themselves trying to understand experiences and concepts far outside of the options available for those of us just a few decades older. As a young girl growing up in the 1960s and 1970s, who was not allowed to wear pants to school until I was in the sixth grade—not on the coldest of New York winter mornings—it is amazing for me to witness the blossoming of diverse gender possibilities for young people today. Decades of progressive politics, spearheaded by feminism and various minority civil rights struggles, and the rise of the gay, lesbian, and bisexual liberation, as well as the current transgender "tipping point," has set the stage for the emergence of this gender revolution. Thanks to these efforts, Gender Quests have simply become a part of adolescence, a normal part of human development.

We are living in an amazing new century, where gender identity—including the complex ways that sex, gender expression, and sexual orientation overlap with gender identity—is being explored by a new generation of visionaries. Young people today are less limited by their biological bodies and surrounding social mores than any previous generation. Like all quest-seekers, they enter the world with a curiosity and bravery unique to youth, who are always the harbingers of social change.

Yet, under the bravado is also fear. Forging one's own identity amidst a world that limits, constrains, and attempts to define youth, constantly telling them that they do not know what is in their minds and hearts, insisting too often that they do not know themselves, is incredibly challenging work. Youth struggle to find the words to explain their experiences to their elders who too easily and too often dismiss these explorations. Brain research tells us that adolescents often think less from their cognitive parts of the brain than from their emotions, which are fierce and strong and volatile. Adolescents will explore themselves with or without adult permission; they will come to their own conclusions about their gender, whether the adults around them support them in their journeys or try to deny them their expression. Grown-ups need to think carefully about how they want to respond to youth if we want to mentor them; we cannot lead them, we can only follow or get out of their way. Clinicians especially are in a powerful position to oppress and dismiss identity exploration; we can also be formidable allies actively mirroring and validating diverse gender expressions, and midwives who nurture the process of birthing new ones.

The Gender Quest Workbook helps youth to focus their exploration; they can do this on their own or with the help of adult guides. It gives them the tools to examine their thoughts and feelings, and opens doors to new ways of seeing themselves and their experiences. It gives them language to help hone their experiences and also give them skills to use this language to talk with adults in their lives—parents, teachers—as well as other teens who may not understand. *The Gender Quest Workbook* recognizes the complexity of dating, of seeking romantic and sexual relationships, while forming a gender identity that feels authentic. A Gender Quest is a road map that is loving, supportive, funny, and educational. It is a rare kind of homework that youth will enjoy doing.

The work of adults—parents and professionals—is to use *The Gender Quest Workbook* ourselves. We cannot begin to mentor youth without understanding the gender possibilities open to them, and how these can both invigorate and overwhelm them. We need to understand our own Gender Quests, and the quests we were forbidden to explore in more repressive times—quests which were prematurely aborted, ridiculed, or punished. We need to do this in order to be fully available without judgment. We need to be conscious of our own unresolved pain, so we can be fully present for this new generation of explorers who have so much to teach us about the outer world and inner realms of gender identity and expression.

Rylan Jay Testa, PhD, is assistant professor in the psychology department at Rhodes College, and research affiliate of the Center for LGBTQ Evidence-based Applied Research (CLEAR). As a clinical psychologist, his research focuses on understanding and preventing self-destructive behaviors and health disparities, particularly among transgender and gender-nonconforming people. He is highly respected for his work in both the field of psychology and in the transgender and gender-nonconforming community.

Deborah Coolhart, PhD, LMFT, is a licensed marriage and family therapist, and assistant professor at the Syracuse University Marriage and Family Therapy program. Her clinical and scholarly work focuses on the strengths and challenges of transgender people and their loved ones, and she has published several journal articles and book chapters on transgender-related topics. Coolhart created a clinical team of master's students who work specifically with transgender clients, their partners, and their families in a free university clinic—providing a valuable service to the transgender community in New York.

Jayme Peta, MA, MS, has been working with and for transgender and gender-nonconforming youth for over fifteen years. Peta holds a master's degree in counseling psychology from Naropa University, and is a doctoral candidate in clinical psychology at Palo Alto University. Peta has given numerous trainings and workshops on working with transgender populations, and taught as an adjunct instructor in Naropa University's psychology department. Peta's current research examines the childhood experiences of transgender adults.

Foreword writer **Ryan K. Sallans, MA**, is a public speaker, diversity trainer, consultant, publisher, and author of the book *Second Son*. Sallans specializes in health care, workplace, and college campus issues surrounding the LGBTQIA community, with a specialized focus on the transgender community. For the past fifteen years, he has worked with organizations and universities on LGBTQ social issues, creating transgender-inclusive environments, and media literacy related to eating disorders, body image, and gender.

Afterword writer **Arlene Istar Lev, LCSW-R, CASAC**, is founder and clinical director of Choices Counseling and Consulting and TIGRIS: The Training Institute for Gender, Relationships, Identity, and Sexuality in Albany, NY. She is a lecturer at the University at Albany, and project director of the Sexual Orientation and Gender Identity Project (SOGI). Istar is also clinical supervisor for Center Support Counseling Services at the Pride Center of the Capital Region. She is author of *The Complete Lesbian and Gay Parenting Guide* and *Transgender Emergence*, winner of the APA Division 44 Distinguished Book Award.

More ⏱ Instant Help Books for Teens

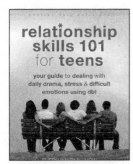

Register your **new harbinger** titles for additional benefits!

When you register your **new harbinger** title—purchased in any format, from any source—you get access to benefits like the following:

- Downloadable accessories like printable worksheets and extra content

- Instructional videos and audio files

- Information about updates, corrections, and new editions

Not every title has accessories, but we're adding new material all the time.

Access free accessories in 3 easy steps:

1. Sign in at NewHarbinger.com (or **register** to create an account).

2. Click on **register a book**. Search for your title and click the **register** button when it appears.

3. Click on the **book cover or title** to go to its details page. Click on **accessories** to view and access files.

That's all there is to it!

If you need help, visit:

NewHarbinger.com/accessories

new harbinger
CELEBRATING
40 YEARS